STEAMBOAT DISASTERS *of the* LOWER MISSOURI RIVER

STEAMBOAT DISASTERS of the LOWER MISSOURI RIVER

Vicki Berger Erwin & James Erwin

Published by The History Press
Charleston, SC
www.historypress.com

Copyright © 2020 by Vicki Berger Erwin and James Erwin
All rights reserved

Front cover, top: State Historical Society of Missouri; *bottom*: U.S. Fish and Wildlife Service. *Back cover*: St. Louis Mercantile Library of the University of Missouri–St. Louis.

First published 2020

Manufactured in the United States

ISBN 9781467143257

Library of Congress Control Number: 2019951836

Notice: The information in this book is true and complete to the best of our knowledge. It is offered without guarantee on the part of the authors or The History Press. The authors and The History Press disclaim all liability in connection with the use of this book.

All rights reserved. No part of this book may be reproduced or transmitted in any form whatsoever without prior written permission from the publisher except in the case of brief quotations embodied in critical articles and reviews.

For our grandchildren: Cameron, Abby, Nora and Charlie.

CONTENTS

Acknowledgements	9
Introduction	11
1. The Missouri River	15
2. The Seeds of Their Own Destruction: The Construction of Missouri River Steamboats	23
3. Safety, Snags and Regulations	35
4. Explosions	49
5. Fire and Ice	63
6. Disease Disasters	71
7. Civil War	77
8. Murders, Revenge, Lynching and Ill-Treatment	91
9. The Uneasy Relationship between Bridges and Steamboats	97
10. Captains and Chroniclers	107
11. Searching for Treasure While Saving History	125
Bibliography	147
Index	155
About the Authors	159

ACKNOWLEDGEMENTS

There are many thanks due to various historical organizations and their people. Everyone at every historical museum and society was so very, very helpful and generous.

We were helped by so many people whom we would like to acknowledge by name. But we seem to have lost the scraps of paper with the chaotic scribbles with that information. We don't want to give some names and omit others. We hope that where we mention institutions and organizations, each individual who reads it will remember us, because we remember you—just not everyone's name.

Missouri State Archives, Jefferson City, Missouri; State Historical Society of Missouri, Columbia, Missouri—a special thanks to staff and archivists who pulled folders for us and emailed photos to us in the middle of preparing for their move to a new facility; Washington Historical Society, Washington, Missouri; Gasconade County Historical Society Archives and Record Center, Hermann, Missouri; Lexington Historical Society, Lexington, Missouri; Roubideaux Row Museum, St. Joseph, Missouri—another special thanks for the best tour ever by the young tour guides; Lafayette County Historical Society, Higginsville, Missouri; Arabia Steamboat Museum, Kansas City, Missouri; St. Charles County Historical Society, St. Charles, Missouri—even without our notes, we remember our friends Louis J. Launer and Linda Prenger, who were so very helpful; Murphy Library Special Collections, University of Wisconsin–La Crosse, La Crosse, Wisconsin—and especially Laura M. Godden, who graciously

Acknowledgements

plucked our tardy request for photos from the bottom of the pile to help us meet our deadlines; Mercantile Library, Herman T. Pott National Inland Waterway Library, University of Missouri–St. Louis; and the DeSoto National Wildlife Refuge and especially Dean Knudsen.

Thanks to Chad Rhoad at The History Press for putting up with our questions, and to Rick Delaney for his expert copyediting on not just this book but all our books he has improved.

INTRODUCTION

In the mid-1990s, Jim and I took a weekend trip to Hannibal, Missouri, where we stumbled upon a small, temporary exhibit of artifacts from an old steamboat that had been uncovered on a farm along the Missouri River. We were fascinated. Jim bought a map showing steamboat wrecks along one small section of the river, and it was hard to believe there were so many. We discussed writing a book about steamboat wrecks, but it wasn't the right time.

When a permanent museum opened in Kansas City, we visited it and learned even more about what we now knew was the steamboat *Arabia*. We were still intrigued and filed it away under "books to write someday."

The day has finally come! And it was every bit as interesting to research steamboats and their disasters as we hoped it would be. So, thank you *Arabia* for setting us on this path. You might be interested to know that the first thing people ask us when we talk about writing a book about steamboat disasters is, "Do you know about the *Arabia*?"

We did expand the definition of "disaster" beyond wrecks. We include disease, fire, explosions, crimes, war and even ice. Our definition of the Lower Missouri River is somewhat expansive, too. St. Louis, a major Mississippi River port, had to be included, because it was the home for nearly all the steamboats plying the Missouri. We set the northern limit at DeSoto, Nebraska, because we wanted to bring in the *Bertrand*, the other Missouri River steamboat that was the subject of extensive excavation and archaeological study.

Introduction

Distances by Water on the Lower Missouri from St. Louis to DeSoto, Nebraska (1869)

Mouth of Missouri River	20	DeWitt	281
St. Charles	45	Miami	286
Augusta	81	Lexington	337
South Point	87	Camden	352
Washington	89	Napoleon	359
Emily Bend	96	Sibley	365
Hermann	118	Missouri City	375
Portland	135	Wayne City	392
Bonnot's Mills	153	Kansas City	405
Mouth of Osage River	156	Parkville	418
Jefferson City	164	Leavenworth	438
Providence	190	Weston	446
Rocheport	204	Atchison	468
Franklin and Boonville	215	St. Joseph	501
Arrow Rock	229	Nebraska City	629
Bluffport	238	Council Bluffs Landing	678
Glasgow	242	Omaha	686
Cambridge	249	Boyer River	706
Frankfort	255	DeSoto	728
Brunswick	274		

There were more than three hundred steamboat wrecks on the Missouri River in the period covered by this book. The stretch between the river's mouth and Kansas City was considered a steamboat graveyard. Of course, we could not write about every wreck. We tried to pick the most interesting and important stories.

One of the problems we encountered in writing this book is that the early steamboat era doesn't have many photos of the boats. Today, if a boat sank on the river, we would have professional news photographs, amateur photos and pictures on Facebook, Twitter and Instagram. We would be drowning in disaster photos. It wasn't as easy to snap a picture in the mid-1800s, and cameras were not nearly so common. We hope you enjoy the images we managed to find.

Introduction

And a bit of advice: If you plan to write a book on the Missouri River, hope it is not a flood year! In 2019, while we were writing about steamboat disasters, there was a flood disaster occurring along the Missouri River. We were unable to reach some of the places we wanted to research, because they were closed or the roads leading to them were closed. We are sorry for the losses these areas and communities suffered.

1
THE MISSOURI RIVER

The Missouri River is the longest river in North America. However, it is impossible to state its exact length, because of its constantly changing nature. Meriwether Lewis and William Clark, on their famous 1804 expedition, calculated the distance of the river at 2,465 miles. But later steamboat men estimated that the river was longer. They claimed it was 3,000 miles from the mouth of the Missouri to Fort Benton, Montana, the practical head of navigation. It was, however, a disadvantage to those steamboat men to have surveyed distances, as shipping costs were based on weight carried per mile. And so, when the course of the river changed—which it did frequently—they could collect more every time a new bend was added. (Of course, they also ran the risk of the river getting shorter when a bend was cut off.)

The first official measurement of distance was set in 1879–91 by army engineers and the Missouri River Commission. That distance was closer to the measurements of Lewis and Clark than to those of the steamboat men: 2,285 miles from the mouth to Fort Benton.

The Missouri River is often divided into the Upper Missouri and the Lower Missouri, due sometimes to geographical differences, to where trade routes begin and end, to historical differences or to characteristics of the river itself. The Upper Missouri is referred to as the "Rocky River," while the Lower is called the "Sandy River." The Rocky River flows over rock and gravel, making the water clearer. The banks are more stable, so the river flows in a straighter line. Many rapids, a steeper slope,

A view of the Missouri River, date unknown. The river is as beautiful as it is dangerous. *Missouri Historical Society.*

shallow chutes and rock ledges make this portion of the river a challenge to navigate.

As the Missouri transitions to the "Sandy River," its banks become less stable and the channel deepens and widens. Many loops and bends are created as a swift current flows easily through the sandy soil. And the sand moves as well as the water, creating even more challenges. Distance between points on the river could be drastically altered by the current's creation of new bends or cutting off old ones. Brunswick, Missouri, for example, was once a river port. A nineteenth-century flood cut it off from the river, and it is now three miles from the Missouri.

On the Lower River, the channel can be deep, but it is usually narrow and seldom runs in a straight line or down the middle. It moves from one side of the river to the other and from the inside of one bend to the outside of the next and then forms an entirely new channel. The bends proved especially dangerous to steamboats and were often named after a boat that sank there. It is precisely because of this difficulty in navigating the Missouri River that good pilots were so highly prized (and paid).

Steamboat Disasters of the Lower Missouri River

As the river speeds along the treelined banks, it eats at those banks, taking soil from one point and depositing it at another. A farmer might fall asleep with a certain acreage and wake up with more due to deposits from the river, or less due to the river washing part of the land away.

Part of the effect of the river's voracious appetite is that it eats away soil around the forests of trees growing along the riverbank. As the trees are "unrooted" and fall away from the bank, they become mired in the riverbed, with the trunks slanting upward, creating the most dangerous of hazards to riverboats and river travel. There are unrooted trees known as "planters" (those firmly fixed and immovable) and "sawyers" (those constantly in motion). Sawyers may be submerged or may rise out of the water with no notice, posing a grave threat to any nearby vessel. Taken together, these types of unrooted trees, plus any other obstruction under the water, are known as snags. More steamboats met disaster due to snags than to all other types of disasters combined.

The Missouri River is also considered the muddiest river on the continent, with 120 tons of sediment suspended in every one million gallons of water. The saying on the river was that the water from the Missouri was "too thin to cultivate and too thick to drink."

Depending on the time of year and the weather conditions, the Missouri River ran high or low. The prime time for steamboat travel (and trade) was when the river ran high, raising the boats above obstructions such as planters and sandbars. The Missouri River usually had two "rises." The spring rise was traditionally in late March, when snow melted on the plains and spring rains were plentiful. This was followed by the June rise, fueled by meltwater from the Rocky Mountains.

When the river iced over in the winter, trips by steamboat were suspended. The boats either "wintered in" or traveled south on the Mississippi to engage in trade on that river or its tributaries. Ice, even when steamboats were docked, posed a danger. When blocks of ice traveled from one point to the other, gathered in one place and froze over, they formed a gorge. When that ice gorge broke up, the shifting of the ice was strong enough to ram boats together or push them on shore, or for the ice blocks to cause their own damage.

Native Americans were long established in villages along the Missouri River, using it as a food and water source and as a natural highway before Europeans "discovered" it.

In 1673, Jesuit missionary Father Jacques Marquette was warned as he traveled along the more tranquil Mississippi River to expect to meet a great river coming in from the west. The Native Americans called it the Pekitanoui, meaning "muddy water." In June, Marquette recorded in his journal:

> *As we were gently sailing down the still clear water* [of the Mississippi], *we heard a noise of a rapid into which we were about to fall. I have seen nothing more frightful, a mass of large trees entire with branches, real floating islands came from Pekitanoui, so impetuous that we could not without great danger expose ourselves to pass across. The agitation was so great that the water was all muddy, and could not get clear.*

Throughout the seventeenth century, other French explorers traveled the Mississippi River, taking note of the Missouri and eventually traveling upriver. The first recorded incidence of a white man ascending the Missouri was in *Travels in North America from 1689 to 1700* by Baron La Houton. He claims to have begun his voyage up the Missouri on March 17, 1699. He met and engaged with Missourie and Osage tribes, reaching the mouth of the Osage River. He returned to the mouth of the Missouri on March 25. The distance traveled by canoe in the time recorded makes it unlikely this trip actually occurred.

The explorer René-Robert La Salle was the one to attach the name *Missouri* to the river, after the Native American tribe the Missourites or Missouries that lived near the mouth of the river.

The Missouri River came into national prominence after the Lewis and Clark expedition in 1804. That exploration shined a light on the opportunities available in the West.

Fur trading had been a prime commercial enterprise from the earliest days of the United States. Fur-bearing animals were abundant in the sparsely settled West in the late eighteenth and early nineteenth centuries, and the Missouri River was a direct route to those furs.

Early trappers and traders traveled—slowly—up the Missouri River by canoes, Mackinaws and keelboats. None of these methods of travel was very efficient or much faster than walking. The arrival of the steamboat could, if it worked on the Missouri River, make a great difference in both travel and trade along the water. It was ten years between the time Robert Fulton's *Clermont* made its successful voyage in the East on August 17, 1807, and the arrival of the first steamboat, the *Zebulon Pike*, in St. Louis, Missouri, on August 2, 1817. And it wasn't until May 1819 that a steamboat, the *Independence*, traveled up the Missouri.

Steamboat Disasters of the Lower Missouri River

This thirteen-day endeavor sponsored by businessmen intent on using steamboats in commerce along the Missouri River was cause for celebration. The *Independence*, carrying passengers and freight, landed at Franklin, Missouri, and the town hosted a grand banquet with food, drinks, speeches and toasts. The party lasted for seven hours. And although it was a grand undertaking, it did not lead to an immediate burgeoning of steamboat trade.

A combination scientific and military expedition was organized by the government to travel up the Missouri River, also in 1819. The scientific expedition would map the river and study flora, fauna, geology and geography. Major Stephen Long led this expedition. The steamboat *Western Engineer* was built expressly for the trip, and an original boat it was. The steamer was a sternwheeler, still novel in the early days of steaming and thought by Long to be better suited to the Missouri River. The boat looked like it was riding on the back of a giant serpent. The bow featured a serpent head that appeared to belch fire and smoke, the chimney having been channeled into it. The body of the serpent lay along the waterline of the boat on both sides, and it had a tail raised over the sternwheel. The boat was designed to awe Native Americans along the way, although it was the size of the vessel and the weapons it carried that proved more terrifying to them.

The *Western Engineer*, one of the first steamboats to journey up the Missouri River, was specially designed to strike awe in the Native Americans. The painting is by C.M. Ismert. *Roubidoux Row Museum, St. Joseph, Missouri.*

The military expedition, to establish and man forts along the Upper Missouri, was separate from Long's expedition, but the two groups intended to travel together.

Five boats were planned for the military expedition; ultimately, only three made it to St. Louis: the *Expedition*, the *Jefferson* and the *Johnson*. None was designed with Missouri River travel in mind.

Both expeditions assumed that they, under government auspices, would initiate steamboat traffic on the Missouri River. As they fell further and further behind their expected departure, they were upstaged by the *Independence* and its May arrival in Franklin, Missouri.

After many delays, Long and the *Western Engineer* finally started its journey up the Missouri River on June 22, 1819, only to be plagued by problems. They finally reached Council Bluffs on September 17, missing their intended destination of the mouth of the Yellowstone River by months and miles.

The military expedition was even later in departing for its journey. The three boats left Fort Bellefontaine at noon on July 5 and took three days to reach St. Charles, Missouri. Only twenty-five miles into the expedition, Colonel Henry Atkinson deserted the boats, deciding to take the soldiers overland.

None of the three military boats reached Council Bluffs. The *Expedition* reached the Martin Cantonment. The *Johnson* made it to a point above Fort Osage. The *Jefferson* was snagged near Cote Sans Dessein, 120 miles from the expedition's starting point. A victim of the first steamboat disaster on the Missouri River, the boat was damaged beyond repair and abandoned. Steamboating on the Missouri River was off to a rocky start.

Initially, steamboat commerce grew slowly. By 1829, increased migration and the resulting growth in population, as well as economic improvement and better steamboats, led to the establishment of a regular packet trade along the Missouri River carrying both passengers and freight.

In the 1830s, Missouri's economy was expanding. In the Boone's Lick area along the river, agriculture was booming. The settlers grew tobacco, hemp, corn, wheat and other farm products. The Santa Fe trade was flourishing, and the fur trade along the Upper Missouri region increased the demand for steamboats.

The need for steamboats to move goods was further boosted in the 1840s and 1850s by westward expansion—the movement of people, including those headed to the California goldfields. Steamboats carried migrants to towns on Missouri's western border, including St. Joseph, Independence and Kansas City, where the travelers stocked up on goods they would need for their overland trek on the Santa Fe, Oregon, California or Mormon trails.

Just at the moment of rising demand for steamboats, a competitor arrived: railroads. Trains could operate year-round, could carry goods and people more cheaply and were more efficient. Some railroads in the early years partnered with steamboat lines to forward traffic westward from where the railroad ended. For example, the Missouri Pacific Railroad had a line from St. Louis to Jefferson City. From there, several steamboats carried freight and passengers west to Weston, Missouri. This arrangement resulted in speedier movement of passengers and goods. But, eventually, rail lines were completed, eliminating the need for steamboats.

Steamboat traffic on the Lower Missouri River was also affected by unsettled conditions in the state of Missouri during the Civil War. Guerrilla attacks, especially in areas sympathetic to the Confederacy, were a constant threat.

Steamboat commerce never truly recovered after the war. Railroads were faster and cheaper. More roads were built. Gasoline engines were coming

During the revetment of the Missouri River, engineers blew up obstructions to clear the way. *Washington Missouri Historical Society.*

into use. Efforts were made to improve the river, removing obstacles and stabilizing the banks to make travel safer and easier, but that did not save steamboat traffic.

The Hermann Ferry and Packet Company was the operator of Missouri's last commercial steamboat. In 1925, the *Hermann* was the only steamboat engaged in trade on the Missouri River. (There were snag boats, dredges and other working steam-powered boats after that date.) In 1935, the company sold the boat, and the purchaser took the boat off the Missouri.

2
THE SEEDS OF THEIR OWN DESTRUCTION

The Construction of Missouri River Steamboats

To residents on the river, its passengers and its crews, the steamboat was a thing of beauty and wonder. It announced its approach by a virtual cannonade of exhaust, emitting smoke from towering chimneys, and by a piercing steam whistle. On his trip to the United States in 1842, Charles Dickens was not nearly as impressed, but his acerbic description of the boat on which he rode was accurate. The steamboat, he wrote, was "foreign to all ideas we are accustomed to entertain of boats," lacking a mast and the usual rigging of a seagoing vessel. It hardly had anything that resembled a stern, sides or a keel.

> *There is no visible deck, even; nothing but a long, black, ugly roof covered with burned-out feathery sparks. Above this towers two iron chimneys, a hoarse escape valve and a glass steerage-house. Then, in order as the eye descends toward the water, are the sides, doors and windows of the staterooms. They are jumbled as oddly together as though they formed a small street built by the varying tastes of a dozen men. The whole is supported on beams and pillars resting on a dirty barge resting just a few inches above the water's edge. And in the narrow space between this upper structure and the barge's deck are the furnace fires and machinery, open at the sides to every wind that blows and every burst of rain the boat encounters along its path.*
>
> *Passing one of these boats at night, one would see the great body of fire, exposed as I have just described, raging and roaring beneath the frail*

pile of painted wood, as well as the machinery not warded off or guarded in any way but doing its work in the midst of the crowd of idlers and migrants and children who throng the lower deck. In addition, the boat would be under the management of reckless men whose acquaintance with its mysteries may have been of just six months' standing. A spectator would feel that the wonder was not that there should be so many fatal accidents, but that any journey should be safely made at all.

The steamboats that plied the Missouri River had little in common with those operating in eastern waters. Although criticized as little more than a collection of "wood, tin, shingles, canvas and twine," the western river steamboat was a remarkable technological achievement. Boats built to eastern designs foundered, and new boats incorporated the features that allowed them to adapt to the unique conditions in which they operated. The Missouri River was swift and strong, alternately deep and shallow (its water level could vary up to thirty-five feet in a few days), rocky in places, sandy in others, full of silt (it earned the name "Big Muddy"), plagued by sandbars and snags, with few cities or towns and no docks. The basic design was settled by trial and error by the mid-1830s and varied little until the development of the internal combustion engine in the twentieth century.

But many elements of the steamboat's design and construction also created vulnerabilities that exposed it to disaster.

Side-wheelers and Stern-wheelers

The most distinctive feature of the Missouri River steamboat was its paddle wheels. Indeed, the most basic classification of such boats was between the side-wheel and the stern-wheel boat. Each had its advantages and disadvantages, but until the Civil War, side-wheelers predominated on the western rivers. (Boats equipped with screw propellers were tried and rejected, because they tended to leak and could not be operated equally effectively forward and backward.)

Locating the paddle on the side of the boat had much to recommend it. Such a boat was more stable than the early stern-wheelers, because the weight was amidships, where the boat was most buoyant; this reduced the stress on the hull. The boilers and engines were just forward of the paddle wheels and allowed shorter steam lines and connecting rods.

Perhaps most important to river operations, the paddle wheels could be run independently. Thus, the pilot could turn the boat quickly by running one wheel forward and the other aft, increasing the vessel's maneuverability in the often-narrow confines of the river's channel. Before the Civil War, insurance companies charged higher fees to insure stern-wheel boats and their cargos.

On the other hand, the side-wheeler's paddle wheels were exposed to driftwood, logs, ice and other debris. They were frequently damaged and required constant repair. Moreover, the large housing and connecting machinery took up valuable cargo deck space and made it difficult for the crew and passengers to move about the boat.

The disadvantages of the side-wheeler were, correspondingly, the advantages of the stern-wheeler. Its paddle wheel was protected from river debris by the hull. The design allowed the hull to be wider and meant far more space for cargo and passengers. The broader beam allowed the boat to have a shallower draft—even with a large cargo—and thus it could penetrate farther up the shallow reaches of the Missouri headwaters and extend its cruising season.

Until advances in design were introduced in the 1850s, the placement of the heavy paddle wheel at the stern stressed the boat's hull and caused it to sag. Moreover, early stern-wheelers were far less maneuverable. Improvements in rudder design and the use of multiple rudders led to the ultimate replacement of side-wheelers with stern-wheelers after the Civil War.

Hulls and Hog Chains

The *Western Engineer* was seventy-five feet long and had a thirteen-foot beam. It had some characteristics that typified steamboats of the "Golden Era," including using a high-pressure engine and drawing only thirty inches. Otherwise, its design reflected conventional ship lines: a deep, well-rounded hull, a heavy frame and a large keel—all necessary to provide stability and control in the deep water of eastern rivers or the ocean but a positive hindrance on the shallow and swift Missouri. The hull housed furnaces, boilers, engines, cargo and passengers below the main deck. Its steering wheel was located aft on a raised quarter deck, and it even sported a mast and sails. Its stern paddle wheel was encased within the lines of the hull. Of course, its most distinctive feature—not copied elsewhere—was the steam vent at the bow in the shape of a serpent.

Within a decade, most of these features disappeared from the western steamboat. To make them commercially viable, steamboats had to be able to make as many trips as possible up the treacherously shallow Missouri River as far as possible. This required increased speed and decreased draft. To accomplish these objectives, builders quickly learned that the trick was to make the boat long and flat-bottomed. The steamboat was not quite a powered box on a barge, but it was close.

The first thing to note about the western river steamboat's hull and superstructure is the most obvious: it was made of wood. While builders of oceangoing ships began to experiment with steel and iron hulls, that development was the antithesis of what was needed on the western rivers: a vessel that was light as possible.

The hulls and their components, such as the keel, stem, sternpost, framing, deck beams and stanchions, were made from white oak. This was a heavy, hard, rot-resistant and shock-resistant wood that was widely available to shipbuilders. The superstructure, decking and bulkheads, on the other hand, were made of white pine or a similar light wood, such as yellow pine or poplar. It was painted or varnished to the owner's taste. Some of the larger boats, particularly on the Mississippi River, were elaborately decorated with intricate gingerbread gilded trim. Such finery was uncommon on the Missouri River, where the boats were primarily intended for freight and passengers migrating to farmlands and mines.

The lightweight, varnished or painted wood of the superstructure was susceptible to fires. And, of course, with the open flames of the furnaces on the main deck, the use of oil lamps and candles by the crew and passengers and the spewing of hot cinders from the chimneys, the danger of fire was always present. Louis Hunter noted that the "thin floors and partitions, light framing and siding, soft and resinous woods, the whole dried out by the sun and wind and impregnated with oil and turpentine from paint, made the superstructure of the steamboat little more than an orderly pile of kindling." Buckets and barrels of water were kept for emergency use. It wasn't until late in the nineteenth century that boats were equipped with pumps for firefighting.

An examination of the *Bertrand* shows the typical steamboat design of the mid-nineteenth century. The *Bertrand* was 162 feet long and 32 feet wide. Its stern wheel extended its length to 178 feet. Its flat-bottomed hull was only 5 feet deep. Because its "water plane area" (the bottom part of the hull that

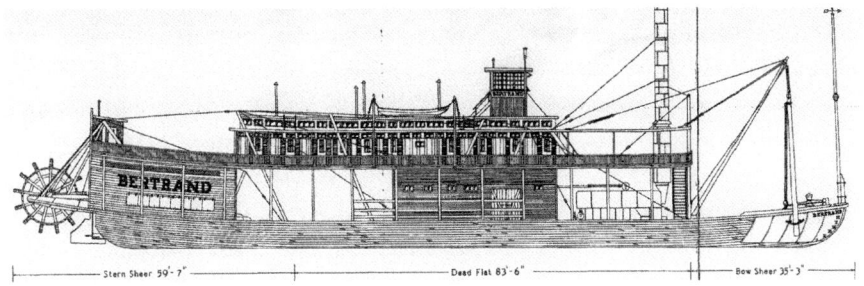

A drawing by Jerry Livingston showing the probable appearance of the *Bertrand*, a typical steamboat of the mid-nineteenth century. *Midwest Archaeological Center, National Park Service.*

sat on the water) was extensive, it drew no more than 4 feet of water even when fully loaded.

It had two decks: the main deck and the boiler deck. (In the idiosyncratic terminology of steamboat design, the boiler was on the main deck and the cabins and pilothouse were on the boiler deck.) The boiler deck's roof was the hurricane deck. It was slightly crowned to shed water and had tar sprinkled with sand to combat the danger from the sparks emitted by the ship's furnaces through the tall chimneys. Larger boats had yet another deck with cabins for the crew, called the Texas deck. (The origin of the name is unknown.) A pilothouse with glass windows sat high above the river for visibility. On some boats, the pilothouse could be as much as fifty feet above the river. A jackstaff—a long pole—was on the bow. It was there to hold a flag and, more importantly, to provide a guide for the pilot in judging location and direction.

The forward deck also had two spars, which could be used to "walk" or "grasshopper" over sandbars. The boat would be driven as far on the sandbar as possible. The spars would be lowered over the bow to a forty-five-degree angle. Lines connected to the spars were wound around the capstan (also located in the bow) until the boat was lifted up and water action washed away some of the sand. When the lines were loosened, the boat would move forward a few feet. It was a tedious process but superior to offloading the cargo and reloading it after the sandbar was passed. Mark Twain compared it to walking on stilts.

The forward main deck was open, with merchandise stacked from one-half to two-thirds of its length. The furnaces and boilers were on the forward third of the main deck, with two large iron chimneys extending well above the pilothouse. Firewood was piled all around the furnaces, leaving a passage for the crew and passengers. The stern paddle wheel was fully exposed. The *Bertrand* had cabins for the passengers and crew on the boiler deck, with doors that opened outward onto a gallery and interior doors that opened into a long dining room. Toilet facilities were located on the upper deck of the stern next to the paddle wheel.

There was no need for masts or sails, and these quickly vanished. Cargo storage was primarily moved to the main deck, and passenger cabins were moved to the upper decks, thus making a shallow hull feasible. The main deck itself was extended to present to the water surface what was essentially a rectangle modified only by the taper of the bow and stern. Even then, later steamboats specially built for the Missouri River trade had bows shaped like a spoon (hence the name "spoonbill" bows) that allowed them to enter ever shallower waters, albeit at the expense of speed. The keel protruding from the bottom of the hull disappeared. A wide beam minimized any tendency to list or roll, an important consideration in the operation of the boilers (as will be seen). Side-wheelers were equipped with guards, or additional decking, that extended beyond the sides of the hull. The guards' primary function was to protect the paddle wheels from ingesting river debris, but they were also used as additional storage space for cargo. Many accounts describe boats "loaded to the guards," meaning the vessel's deck was only (as Dickens observed) a few inches above the river's current.

The bowsprit, with its sometimes-elaborate figure seen on sailing ships, was not only unnecessary but also a positive hindrance. Because there were few, if any, docks on the Missouri River, steamboats had to land against the shore. Typically, the pilot would land the vessel with its bow against the shore pointed upstream. (Landing it with the bow pointed downstream was called a "French landing" and made it more difficult to re-enter the channel.) Deckhands would manhandle ramps that extended from the deck to the shore for the loading and unloading of passengers and cargo. Having the main deck virtually at water level made cargo handling easier and relieved the crew of the necessity of using cranes.

The principal structural problem created by the long, flat steamboat hull was maintaining its longitudinal strength. Without some method of reinforcement, the hull would "hog" and sag—it would hump up in the center, the ends would droop and the sides would also droop. One of the most important innovations in steamboat design was the development of the "hog chain." Hog chains were a series of metal rods connected by turnbuckles that connected the bow and stern and the sides of the boat. The turnbuckles had to be frequently tightened to keep the hull in proper alignment. If the hog chains were broken by striking a sandbar or other obstacle, it could result in the vessel's back being broken and making it suitable only for salvage.

Steamboat men were quite proud of the ability of their vessels to carry large cargos in shallow water, giving rise to numerous colorful descriptions of their capabilities. Mark Twain famously declared that they could sail on "a heavy dew." George Fitch was quoted as saying that steamboats "must be so built that when the river is low and the sandbars come out for air, the first mate can tap a keg of beer and run the boat four miles on the foam."

Boilers, Doctors and Death Hooks

Engines and boilers on western steamboats evolved quickly, again in response to river conditions. Early steamboats used a low-pressure engine. They had much to recommend them. Low-pressure engines were safer and more economical than high-pressure engines. But compared to high-pressure engines, they were heavy, expensive, required a more skilled engineer and were far more susceptible to clogged pipes and flues resulting from the silty water of western rivers. Perhaps most important, the low-pressure engine lacked the reserve "wad of power" needed to operate on rivers with strong currents, twisting channels and numerous sandbars or other obstructions that had to be avoided or simply plowed through. The high-pressure steam engine was simple, compact, lightweight, easy to operate and (an important consideration on the frontiers served by the Missouri River) easy to repair. They were also more dangerous.

The basic design of steamboat boilers and engines was settled by the mid-1830s. The standard boiler was a cylindrical, horizontal tube about thirty feet long with a firebox at one end. Firebricks enclosed a firebox from thirty-six to forty-two inches in diameter. The boiler had two internal flues that carried hot gasses through the boiler to heat the water that was used to create steam. Boilers were made of wrought-iron plates curved and riveted together with the joints staggered to provide greater strength and had cast-iron heads. As time went on, boats were built with a battery of boilers—some having as many as ten to operate its engines. At least two engines were ideal to be able to run a side-wheeler's paddle wheels independently of each other. Of course, more engines also meant more power, but that had to be balanced against the extra weight.

Steamboat Disasters of the Lower Missouri River

The boilers had to be cleaned frequently—as often as every fifteen hours on the Missouri River—because the water used to make steam came from the muddy river itself. It was a nasty job. George Merrick wrote of his experience when still a boy:

> One of my duties was to creep into the boilers through the manhole, which was just large enough to let me through; and with a hammer and a sharp-linked chain I must "scale" the boilers by pounding on the two large flues and sides with the hammer and sawing the chain around the flues until all the accumulated mud and sediment was loosened.

No doubt spurred on by engineers and their assistants disgusted by the task of cleaning boilers, designers created blowout valves that got rid of much of the muck by discharging it into mud drums underneath.

Two chimneys extended from the furnace far above the deck, as high as forty to sixty feet or more above the water. This posed a problem when bridges across the Missouri River became common, requiring hinged chimneys. (What we might call smokestacks were always described as chimneys by steamboat men.) High chimneys were essential to create a natural draft for the fires and to carry away smoke, soot and cinders.

Steamboats on the Missouri River burned huge amounts of wood. Fortunately for the industry, wood was abundant along much of their routes. Woodyards sprang up all along the river to supply the hungry fires of steamboats. The crews had to load enough wood in all kinds of weather and conditions, day and night, to ensure that the vessel could make it to the next fueling point. Some deck passengers could earn a discount on their fare if they pitched in to help.

The most feared and most spectacular steamboat disaster was the boiler explosion. Boiler explosions were almost invariably the result of poor water management. When the water in the boiler became low, the flues became red hot and malleable. If the flues failed, hot gasses were introduced into the boiler, and the steam pressure exceeded the ability of the boiler to contain it.

The need for a surge of power leaving a landing sometimes led the captain and engineer to skirt the limits of safety by introducing cold water into the boiler, which immediately turned into steam. But too much steam pressure could blow up the boiler, scalding whoever was unlucky enough to be nearby if the explosion itself did not kill them. This is one likely explanation of many boiler explosions, particularly those that happened just after the boat was leaving the landing. Fully two-thirds of boiler explosions occurred during this event.

Given the importance of keeping enough water in the boiler, it is not out of place to ask how this could be allowed to happen. It sometimes resulted from mere inattention. Sometimes, the ship's fires were not properly banked, and the blazes became too hot at a time when little or no water was being added to the boilers. The boat may also have careened or listed while being loaded and unloaded, causing the water in the boiler to shift correspondingly, exposing the flues. A similar effect could be achieved if the passengers crowded to one side to say farewell to those on shore or simply to watch the crew casting off the lines to shore.

Of course, another cause of boiler explosions was simply building fires that were too hot and increasing the steam pressure beyond what the boiler could contain. The demand for additional power to combat strong currents or to make up delays sometimes led captains, pilots and engineers to take chances that resulted in disaster.

Despite many innovations to address problems presented by the operation of steamboats on the western rivers, there was strangely little early effort to make or improve steam gauges. The usual way to check the water level in a boiler was through gauge cocks or "try cocks." These were simply three valves in the boiler, one at the normal water level, one a few inches above and another a few inches below that level. Maritime historian Adam Kane described their operation: The try cocks were opened with a gauge stick, usually a broomstick. If water flowed from the top gauge, the supply was cut off; if water flowed from the middle one, the supply was normal; if water only flowed from the lower one, water was added. If all three were dry, "there followed a guessing match as to just how far below the minimum the water really was." It was, at best, a crude measure of the boiler's water level and could lead to misleading results, because just opening the try cocks could cause the water in the boiler to foam, "giving a false impression of its level."

Supplying water to the boilers depended on the engines running a small feedwater pump. When the boat stopped and the fires were still burning, the feedwater pump stopped as well. This, of course, could lead to low water in the boiler or even worse—a boiler explosion. The captain had few options to avoid disaster, none of which was particularly desirable: bank the fires (which required stoking them up again to provide sufficient steam), keep the paddle wheels turning slowly or move the vessel in a circle while trying to load and unload passengers and cargo, or disconnect the engine from the paddle wheels and re-connect them only when ready to leave the landing just to run a small pump. The solution was the addition of an auxiliary steam-powered pump that drove a flywheel. Steam was bled off the boiler into a vertical cylinder that ran a pump drawing water from the river. Then the water would be heated and injected into the boiler, providing a steady stream that—at least in theory—kept the water level at the proper level. It was called a "doctor" because the hope was that it would cure the ills caused by low water in the steamboat's boilers. The doctor also ran bilge pumps and supplied the hoses. All but the smallest boats had a doctor by the 1850s.

The engines had safety valves that, at least in river lore, seemed to be ignored as often as they were used. The safety valve was held down by a moveable weight on a lever called the "death hook." An engineer could either put weight on the death hook or wedge it down with a board to increase the steam pressure being generated for the engines. Lacking a reliable steam gauge, this practice was extremely dangerous and led to demands that the safety valves be designed so that an engineer could not tamper with it.

The final distinctive feature of the western river steamboat was the paddle wheel. These could be enormous, with their housing extending as high as the boiler deck. The side-wheeler's housing was often painted with the vessel's

The "doctor" and boilers of the *Arabia*. *Author photo. Arabia Steamboat Museum.*

The safety valve and "death hook" of the *Arabia*. *Author photo. Arabia Steamboat Museum.*

name, the name of the company that operated it and fancy decorations, such as flowers. The paddles were cheap to build and easy to repair, which was fortunate, because they were often damaged by river debris or ice hundreds of miles from any shipyard. The paddle wheel's principal drawback was its weight—always a consideration in trying to build a boat that had to traverse shallow riverbeds.

The steamboats that operated on the Missouri River were cheap to build and built cheaply. They certainly were not built to last. The average life span of a Missouri River steamboat was three years, about half the average age of Mississippi River boats.

Steamboats were, as Louis Hunter described them, "limber." The hulls flexed, boilers would "pant"—visibly expand and contract—and the engines would emit an explosive exhaust accompanied by "creaking, groaning, pounding of machinery laboring under a heavy load." Despite its defects, the steamboat fulfilled the transportation needs of the mid-nineteenth century. They were of low cost and easy to build and repair. In addition, they were adapted to conditions found on the Missouri River, where there was, George Fitch wrote, "a low grade of fuel, a low grade of water, and a low grade of management."

3

SAFETY, SNAGS AND REGULATIONS

Although the dangers encountered in steamboat operations were well known, in keeping with nineteenth-century political philosophies, the federal government regulated steamboats with a light hand. Regulations requiring the inspection of vessels were not passed until 1838, following a series of spectacular explosions on the Ohio and Mississippi Rivers. The early attempts at regulation improved matters, but not by much, leading to the passage of a more comprehensive law in 1852. Further legislation in 1871 filled in some of the lacunae left by antebellum regulations.

Although boiler explosions grabbed the headlines, the principal threats to commerce on the Missouri and other western rivers were obstructions to navigation, natural and man made. Steamboats had to dodge snags, logs, driftwood, boulders, sand and gravel bars, rock shoals and even sunken boats. In later years, they had to deal with the problems caused by bridges. But removing these obstacles created another national controversy: the decades-long struggle over the federal government's role in internal improvements.

Boiler Explosions Force Congress to Address the Dangers of Steam Power

Although snags, fire, disease and other less dramatic events were the workaday dangers faced by steamboats, boiler explosions were the accidents that captured the public's attention and finally led to the first federal efforts to regulate commerce on the western rivers. In the 1820s and 1830s, there was a steady trickle of such disasters, but none of the scale reached in a few brief weeks in 1838.

On April 25, 1838, the *Moselle* left the wharf at Cincinnati to pick up a few passengers waiting at a nearby town. Apparently desiring to impress the citizens by racing back past the city, the captain and engineer did not bank the fires during this brief stop and tied down the safety valve to keep the vessel's steam pressure up. But after only one revolution of the paddle wheels, when the boat pulled away from the bank, three of the *Moselle*'s four boilers exploded, sending a cloud of smoke, steam, debris and bodies into the air. At least 150 persons were killed. Then, word of the explosion of the *Oronoko*'s boilers on the Mississippi River with 100 deaths reached the rest of the country. Still reeling from these disasters, the country learned of a third boiler explosion, this time on the *Pulaski* on eastern waters.

A previously lethargic Congress sprang into action to provide for "the better security of the lives of passengers." The Steamboat Act of 1838 required all steamboats to be licensed. Their hulls, boilers and machinery were to be inspected periodically and certified as sound. The owners were required to employ competent and skillful engineers. (An amendment that would have required that each vessel have an experienced engineer on board at all times was defeated because, it was said, there weren't enough experienced engineers in the country to comply with the proposed law.) A vessel was required to open its safety valves when at a landing or wharf to keep the steam pressure from building to a dangerous level. Officers and crew could be fined or imprisoned for negligence resulting in the loss of life.

All these provisions sounded impressive, but historians acknowledge that the 1838 statute was an abysmal failure. While boilers were to be inspected, they were not required to undergo a hydraulic test, the only means to determine whether they were of adequate strength. The inspectors were appointed by federal district judges—hardly people inherently qualified to select knowledgeable persons. The inspectors were not supervised or given any uniform standards to follow in carrying out their duties. The system was, as Louis Hunter pointed out, "condemned by steamboatmen as superficial and incomplete and described in later government reports as mere farce." Its principal beneficial effect was to establish the principle that the federal government could regulate steamboat commerce.

Congress returned to the subject with the Steamboat Act of 1852. This statute corrected many of the deficiencies of the earlier statute but only applied to vessels carrying passengers. Freight boats continued to be regulated by the 1838 act. The later statute required hydrostatic tests of boilers and established a maximum allowed steam pressure. Firehoses and lifeboats were required, and the vessel was required to provide an adequate means of escape for deck passengers. Pilots and engineers were required to pass an examination to be licensed. The law also allowed pilots and engineers to overrule the captain's orders if he directed them to engage in unsafe practices. An effective inspection system was created, with competent inspectors who were given not only the authority to license boats, pilots and engineers, but also the authority to revoke their licenses. The president appointed a national board to supervise the local inspectors.

The final piece of federal regulation came in 1871. This law required captains to be licensed and provided protections for the crew as well as the passengers.

The 1852 law helped to reduce fatalities even as more and more steamboats were built. The boiler explosions that occurred in the first few years after its passage, for example, were limited to boats built before 1852, to which its boiler inspection provisions did not apply. While no law, however well administered, could prevent all accidents, the 1852 statute was certainly an improvement over its predecessor.

Snags and "Uncle Sam's Toothpullers"

In 1897, Captain Hiram M. Chittenden of the Army Corps of Engineers prepared a report on the causes of steamboat sinkings on the Missouri River. While boiler explosions, such as that of the *Saluda*, earned newspaper headlines, there were only a handful of those on the river. By far the most common cause of steamboat accidents was snags—193 of 295 wrecks, 65 percent of all sinkings. The next highest causes were fires and ice—24 each, or less than 20 percent of all causes. There were only 6 boiler explosions, but the casualties from each of those calamities were higher than those from any single snag accident.

The Missouri River was full of driftwood. Tree limbs and other debris collected on sandbars and caused more debris to accumulate. Steamboats could overcome these obstacles by avoiding the sandbars or simply by pushing through them. The more dangerous and insidious obstacle was the snag. Snags were trees that had fallen into the river, usually from the periodic floods that ripped them from the bank. "Tossed and battered against riverbank and river bed," Louis Hunter wrote, "the drifting trees lost most of their limbs and branches and, through the absorption of water, much of their buoyancy as well. Their root balls would be weighed down by cobbles and dirt and the trees sink to the bottom of the river, there to become embedded in the sand and gravel....With its trunk inclined upward like a lance the snag lay ready to impale any vessel that came its way." Snags could punch a hole in the boat's hull that would sink it in minutes. In low water, snags could be seen and avoided, but in high water, it took a sharp eye from the pilot to find them, if they could be seen at all. Even a boat drawing five feet or less could be sunk when it hit a massive tree trunk concealed just under the surface.

The federal government made sporadic efforts to remove snags and improve navigation on the western rivers, but funding was caught up in a decades-long political fight over internal improvements—a debate that dominated national politics until the festering sore of slavery intensified in the 1850s. Most of the federal budget in the antebellum years was devoted to the military. Politicians fought over the scraps and frequently resorted to allocation of funds for the improvement of rivers and harbors on a proportional basis. Paul Paskoff noted that in 1852, for example, Congress appropriated 37 percent of the money for specific river and harbor improvements to the Mississippi, Ohio and Missouri Rivers—the precise

A "giant snag" being removed by the snag boat *Wright*, showing the large root ball that anchored it to the bottom of the river. *State Historical Society of Missouri, Columbia, Missouri.*

A typical nineteenth-century government snag boat operating on the western rivers. Harper's Weekly, *November 2, 1880.*

proportion of the nation's population that lived there. Nevertheless, it seemed much easier to get funds for a lighthouse on the coast than for a project on the western rivers—perhaps because, as Ambrose Bierce said, a lighthouse was a "tall building on the seashore in which the government maintains a lamp and the friend of a politician." (Although authorized by the 1838 law, navigation lights were not installed on western rivers until the 1870s.) But proportionality of population was hardly the gauge of need. During the prewar period (1821–62), Missouri, for example, received far less in funds than nine other states, none of which had as many as two-thirds of the steamboat wrecks as occurred within Missouri's borders.

Specially designed snag boats provided the principal method to remove snags. Snag boats had double hulls with a crane in the middle. They were ruggedly built, with a heavy beam that joined the hulls at the bow. The snag boat ran at full power toward a snag and caught it on the beam, lifting it out of the water. It was then raised up by the crane and cut up. The stump and root ball were usually dumped back into the river or carried to shore.

Steamboat Disasters of the Lower Missouri River

Snag boats, nicknamed "Uncle Sam's Toothpullers," could remove a snag weighing up to seventy-five tons. A second and cheaper method of snag removal was to prevent the trees from becoming snags altogether. Part of the boat's crew would be put ashore with axes and saws to cut down the trees lining the banks before the water could sweep them into the river.

The magnitude of the task was daunting. From August 1, 1844, to the close of the year, the snag boats *Sevier* and *Samson* removed 3,425 snags and 253 logs and cut 653 trees from the mouth of the Missouri River to Weston, Missouri.

The government reported that on the entire Mississippi and Missouri River system (including tributaries) between 1842 and 1845, it removed 21,681 snags, 36,840 roots, logs and stumps and 74,910 trees judged liable to fall into the rivers. Elimination of snags was a never-ending task. Between 1868 and 1884, snag boats removed an average of 2,872 snags annually weighing an average of sixteen tons each from the Mississippi, Missouri and Arkansas Rivers.

Yet another hazard that needed to be removed from the riverbeds were sunken boats—steamboats, barges and flatboats. Steamboatmen were the original recyclers. If a boat could not be raised, salvors removed not only the salvageable cargo but also the boat's engines, furniture and as much of its superstructure and hull as could be saved, all of which was either sold at auction or used in a new boat. Sometimes, the entire hull was raised and used in a new boat. Such items could be used over and over again. It was not unusual for engines to be used in as many as four boats before they finally wore out. For obvious reasons, the re-use of boilers was dangerous and rarely done.

Insurance companies and boat owners hired specialists either to raise or to salvage sunken boats. They could work quickly, depending on river conditions. By the 1850s, a boat that sank in the morning could be raised by the afternoon if the requisite vessel equipped with strong steam pumps and siphons happened to be nearby. With the water pumped out of the boat, the salvors could install temporary bulkheads to seal the hole in the hull sufficiently to allow the boat to have more permanent repairs made. In a ten-year period, the *T.F. Eckert*, a salvage boat owned by the Cincinnati Underwriters, successfully raised or removed 360 wrecked steamboats and other vessels while recovering 20,000 tons of machinery and cargo.

If the boat sank in deep water but was still capable of being raised, salvors used a diving bell or a diving suit to reach it. James B. Eads entered the salvage business using what he called "bell boats." Eads later used techniques

The *T.F. Eckert*. Owned by an insurance company, it was hired to salvage 360 steamboats and other vessels in a ten-year period. *Murphy Library Special Collections, University of Wisconsin–La Crosse, La Crosse, Wisconsin.*

developed from salvaging sunken steamboats to protect workers building the piers dug deep into the Mississippi River for the Eads Bridge in St. Louis.

Some of the early steamboats that met with ultimate disaster had an interesting previous "life" often plagued by pre-disasters in which they were sunk and raised, often multiple times. Their stories illustrate some of the many adventures a steamboat could have.

THE *MOLLIE DOZIER*

The *Mollie Dozier*, captained by Fred Dozier and named for his wife, entered the Missouri River trade in the spring of 1865. It was one of those boats that had a short but exciting life on the river.

At some point in the *Mollie Dozier*'s short life, probably in 1865, it was attacked by guerrillas while tied up taking on wood in northern Missouri. When the gang of men swarmed the boat, Captain Dozier knew better than to try to resist. His crew wasn't armed (for fear of mutiny), and there were too many guerrillas. Once the gang of ruffians was on board, they headed first for the liquor and drank their fill. When they'd had enough, they filled their saddlebags with what was left and directed their attention to the pantry. They ate their fill and carried the remaining food ashore. The leader, a big man with a red beard, ignored the food and drink and went for the safe, clearing it out. The leader then told Captain Dozier that he and his band of men would leave as soon as the captain turned over the Yankee on board. Captain Dozier did have a Union soldier headed home on furlough on the boat. But he acted as though he didn't know who or what the guerrilla leader was talking about. Before the situation could grow more tense, the men found the soldier and dragged him out of his stateroom. To the horror of Captain Dozier, the crew and passengers, the leader of the bushwhackers tied the soldier to the pommel of his saddle and rode away, dragging the soldier behind him.

In August that same year, the *Leavenworth Times* reported a crime aboard the *Dozier*. Aaron Stewart, a discharged Union soldier, boarded the steamer headed downstream. When he disembarked, his carpet bag was left behind. Before the bag could be returned to the former soldier, an unknown person broke into it and took $302, the entirety of Stewart's savings from his service in the army.

But that wasn't the end of the story. According to W.H. Black, clerk of the *Mollie Dozier*, in a letter to the *Leavenworth Times*, the report was untrue and made only to damage the steamboat's reputation. Black recounts that Stewart boarded at Leavenworth and had only ten dollars toward his passage. He promised to pay the remainder on reaching St. Louis. He turned his valise over to a cabin boy upon boarding. At Kansas City, both Stewart and the cabin boy left the boat and were not seen again until Stewart appeared in St. Louis asking for his luggage. He then declared his money stolen.

Black said that passengers were invited to place their money in the safe aboard the *Mollie Dozier*; if they chose not to do so, the boat would not be held responsible for its loss. He questioned whether any money was ever in the valise, as Stewart had strongly indicated he had only ten dollars when he came on board. No resolution to the case was reported.

Early in the 1866 season, the *Mollie Dozier* caught fire while docked in St. Louis. Fire engines were called, but the fire was extinguished by the crew before they could arrive. The blaze started in tarps covering furniture on board, and damage was slight.

That same year, on the season's first trip upriver, the *Dozier* was headed out at the same time as the newly minted *Wm. J. Lewis* for Fort Benton, Montana Territory. By then, the *Mollie Dozier* was a respected steamboat, known for its speed and dependability. The *Lewis* was a large boat, 215 feet long and 36 feet wide. The *Dozier* was a similar size at 225 feet long and 34 feet wide. Although not officially racing, both captains, Frank Dozier on the *Dozier* and Ed Herndon on the *Lewis*, knew the first boat to arrive would have a distinct trade advantage.

Both steamboats were scheduled to leave at noon on March 27, 1866. The *Wm. J. Lewis*, loaded with 260 tons of freight, left at 4:30 p.m. that day, but the *Mollie Dozier* was delayed until the next day to finish loading its 240 tons of cargo.

The *Wm. J. Lewis* cruised along without a sighting of the *Mollie Dozier* until April 15, when the *Dozier* passed it. At that point, the *Lewis*'s pilot, Captain Carrol Jones Atkins, headed for a cutoff channel and came out ahead of the *Dozier*. Above Vermilion, South Dakota, the two steamers approached an island in the middle of the river. The *Lewis* went right, and the *Dozier* headed left. The *Mollie Dozier* gained a two-and-a-half-mile lead with its choice.

The boats steamed along, one ahead, then the other. The *Mollie Dozier* liked to wait until the *Wm. J. Lewis* was stopped to take on wood, steaming past and giving a toot on its whistle.

The *Wm. J. Lewis* caught up to the *Dozier* and pulled ahead—directly into an ice field. The floating ice smashed its paddle blades, and the boat had to stop for repairs. Once it was on its way, the *Lewis* passed the *Mollie Dozier* run aground. Fortunately for the *Dozier*, it rained, and it floated off the bar and back into the lead, only to become stuck on another sandbar. This time, it had to use its spars to "grasshopper" over and off.

The *Lewis* lost that lead when the winch line it was using to move up a channel over rapids broke. It was bad news for both steamers. The strong current pushed the *Lewis* back and right into the *Mollie Dozier*, damaging them both.

The *Wm. J. Lewis* finished its repairs first and arrived at Fort Benton on May 31 at 4:30 a.m., beating the *Mollie Dozier*'s time by thirty-three hours and forty-five minutes.

The *Lewis*, after a nine-week trip upriver, headed back to St. Louis on June 2, having made $60,000 on its maiden voyage, equal to the entire cost of the steamboat.

The big boat race was not the only excitement encountered by the *Mollie Dozier* that year. On June 13, it was struck by hostile fire from the Sioux tribe at the mouth of the Little Muddy River. The *Bismarck Tribune*, in a retrospective article about Indian attacks on steamboats on the Missouri River, tells an enhanced version of the story. The captain's wife and his young child were traveling with him on the trip, and all were in the pilothouse with Tom Campbell. Lew Lorrain was at the wheel. The article reports that about 150 hostiles attacked, and no fewer than fifty bullets went through the pilothouse, yet no one was harmed. Captain Dozier grabbed his child and departed via the stairs. Campbell jumped through a window on the side away from the Indians and caught hold of a hog chain to hold himself on board. Lorrain stayed at the wheel until a second volley hit. He tied off the wheel and also exited via the window. No mention is made of what measures Mrs. Dozier took.

Despite losing the race to the *Wm. J. Lewis* and being attacked by Indians, the *Mollie Dozier* had a good 1866 season, netting $50,000 from the Missouri River trade.

On October 3, 1866, at 11:00 a.m., disaster struck the *Mollie Dozier* for the last time. It struck a snag on its way downriver just below St. Mary's (near present-day Portland, Missouri) and sank with no loss of life. The boat was left in about six feet of water, and it was initially believed that it could be raised. On October 10, the Louisville *Courier-Journal* reported that the boat had broken in two and could not be salvaged. Attempts were made nonetheless by Submarine No. 13. Bulkheads were built around the *Mollie Dozier*, but the fear of ice and cold weather resulted in abandonment of the raising. The bend where the steamboat lay was known going forward as the *Mollie Dozier* chute.

The *New Lucy*

Some of the steamboats that met a disastrous end had interesting, though one might say unlucky, lives before they disappeared from the river.

Early in its career, in January 1853, the *New Lucy* caught fire while docked at the St. Louis levee, foreshadowing its eventual fate. Once on fire, the *New Lucy* burned through its ropes and would have set more boats on fire if the captain of the nearby *Altona* had not had the foresight to haul it to the nearby Bloody Island. Only the hull of the *Lucy* survived, but it was rebuilt over the winter and back on the water by spring.

The *New Lucy*, a stern-wheeler built in 1852, gained a reputation for being not only a "floating palace" but also exceptionally fast. One of the traditions among steamboats on the Missouri was for the fastest boat on the river to display a pair of silver-tipped elkhorns on the front of the boat. The tradition started in St. Joseph, Missouri, with the *Polar Star*. On the *New Lucy*'s trial trip from St. Louis to St. Joseph in July 1853, it was on track to acquire those horns. It left St. Louis on July 8, planning to travel straight through to St. Joseph without landing. The *New Lucy* was setting records when one of its boilers burned just past Boonville, Missouri. The boat continued to Glasgow, Missouri, where, despite its troubles, it beat the prior fastest time on record (St. Louis to Glasgow), thirty-one hours and seven minutes, set by the *Polar Star*. The *New Lucy*'s time came in—with the damaged boiler—at thirty hours and fourteen minutes, cutting fifty minutes off the record.

For this record-setting trip, the *New Lucy* set out with 160 cords of wood on board (equal to 160 tons of freight). As the wood was consumed, its speed increased. Captain Conley of the *Lucy* said it "would undoubtedly have taken the horns" but for the disastrous accident. Even the rival Captain Brierly of the *Polar Star* had confidence that the *New Lucy* would break his record. He left the horns in St. Joseph "just in case."

The rivalry between the two boats continued. In June 1854, the *New Lucy* made the trip from St. Louis to Glasgow in the fastest time of the season—until the *Polar Star* arrived a few days later with an even faster time. Fast arrivals meant more than bragging rights and the honor of displaying horns. It meant growth of the boat's reputation and the ability to take on waiting shipments before the next boat arrived. Merchants were always looking for faster delivery of their goods.

On October 2, 1854, the *New Lucy* met with more trouble. The steamer left St. Louis and encountered rain and wind bad enough to compel it to land a few miles below Jefferson City. A letter to the editor of the *Glasgow Weekly Times* from a *New Lucy* passenger describes what happened next:

> *The cabin of the boat was almost totally wrecked. There were several carriages on the hurricane roof, which together with the meat house and chicken coop, went overboard. The chimneys followed next. Then the hurricane deck, as far back as the chimneys, fell with a crash, and about the same time the starboard side of the cabin gave way, and the rooms as far back as the wheel-house, were unroofed, leaving the inmates exposed to the torrents of rain that was [sic] falling. The pantry together with the ware that was hanging upon it, was carried some forty yards on the shore. There were some ninety passengers on the boat, and the scene that followed beggars description, everybody was sound asleep, and upon being awakened under such circumstances, great alarm and confusion prevailed.....No one received any material injury.*

The *Kate Swinney* took the passengers aboard the next morning. The amount of damage to the *New Lucy* as a result of the storm amounted to $3,000. The carriages blown from the hurricane deck were the only freight losses.

Another custom on the river was to present gifts and awards to favored boats and captains. On a "pleasure party" trip upriver from Weston, Missouri, to St. Joseph, complete with a band, dancing, "social chat" and refreshments, Captain Conley of the *New Lucy* was so honored, indicating what a popular boat the *Lucy* was. He received a pair of engraved silver cups, and his clerks, mates and steward also received silver cups. To top it off, Captain Conley's daughter received a pony!

On March 15, 1857, the *New Lucy* struck a snag above Cambridge, Missouri, knocking a hole in its hull. It ran aground on a sandbar and filled with water. The boat was raised and repaired. Later in 1857, on September 26, the *New Lucy* sank yet again a few miles above Miami, Missouri. It was once again raised and repaired. The *New Lucy*'s final disastrous chapter occurred on November 22, 1857. It was totally destroyed by fire while laid up by ice opposite DeWitt, Missouri. No lives were lost, but the big steamboat that seemed indestructible collected insurance of $12,000.

Twentieth-Century Wrecks—The *Missouri* and the *Kappa*

River obstructions were much less of a problem in the twentieth century, but occasionally, unseen sunken objects could end a boat's life, even the life of a snag boat.

The snag boat *Missouri* cleared the Missouri River of snags for many years. Who could have predicted that its ultimate end was to become one of those obstructions? The boat was, in 1928, the largest craft working the river. Only one steamer, the *Hermann*, was working in river trade by then. Towboats and barges had taken over. The crew of the *Missouri* numbered forty people, including maids, laundresses, cooks, a blacksmith, engineers, firemen and deckhands. The boat was captained by John S. Campbell. It had worked in the months preceding its disaster taking business leaders and officials on cruises along the river to show them the progress being made on the Missouri River reclamation project, in part a project to revive river navigation.

Steamboat Disasters of the Lower Missouri River

Top: The *Missouri*, a U.S. snag boat, was the largest craft working on the Missouri River in the early part of the twentieth century. *Washington Missouri Historical Society*.

Middle: The *Kappa* served as a government dredge boat on the Missouri River in the early part of the twentieth century. *Washington Missouri Historical Society*.

Bottom: On March 3, 1930, the *Kappa* sank after striking the sunken snag boat *Missouri*. *Washington Missouri Historical Society*.

Steamboat Disasters of the Lower Missouri River

On the evening of Friday, July 27, 1928, the *Missouri* tied up at the mouth of the Gasconade River. There were thirty-eight people on board when a fire broke out at 3:30 a.m. The fire (whose cause was unknown) spread quickly, making it necessary for the crew to escape, leaving behind all personal items.

One crew member, the cook, known only as Maggie, died. She was believed to be aboard the lifeboat headed for shore until she cried out for help. The lifeboat quickly returned, pulling as close to the burning *Missouri* as possible and calling to her to jump. Whether she turned back out of confusion and fear or to reclaim personal items, the woman perished in the flames.

The boat was cut loose to prevent nearby vessels from catching fire. The *Missouri* was completely destroyed, resulting in a loss of $200,000.

Less than two years later, on March 3, 1930, a government dredge boat, the *Kappa*, was on its way to St. Charles when it struck the sunken *Missouri*. No one on the *Kappa* was hurt, but the boat was a complete loss valued at $178,000. The *Kappa* had served on the Missouri River for twenty-eight years.

4

EXPLOSIONS

Although explosions are without a doubt the most attention-grabbing of all steamboat disasters, they did not occur that often. This is fortunate, because they were also the deadliest of all disasters.

THE *EDNA*

The *Edna* set out from St. Louis on July 2, 1842, bound up the Missouri with a full load of freight and a number of immigrants from Germany on board as deck passengers. It tied up near the mouth of the Missouri next to the *Iatan* about 1:00 a.m. At 4:15 a.m. on July 3, the *Iatan* cast off; the *Edna* followed shortly after. It had not gotten more than one hundred feet from the shore when the two flues in the larboard (left) boiler collapsed, spewing steam on the main deck. Thirty-three of the Germans died that day. Another eleven to twenty-two (accounts differ) died within the next month. Only deck passengers were killed or injured.

Captain N.J. Eaton of the *Iatan* noted that the *Edna*'s engines were working out of gear for at least a half hour before it shoved off and that the engines had not stopped for more than ten minutes. He concluded that some sort of stoppage that clogged the water-supply pipes to the boilers—likely silt or vegetable matter sucked into them—caused the water in the boiler to become low and its flues to collapse. A coroner's jury later agreed with Captain Eaton's analysis and held the chief engineer guilty of culpable neglect or bad management.

THE *BIG HATCHIE*

The *Big Hatchie* was one of the few stern-wheelers operating on the Missouri River in 1845. It left St. Louis on July 21 bound for St. Joseph under the command of Captain Roswell R. Frisbee. In addition to freight and a few cabin passengers, it had many German immigrants on board as deck passengers. At 1:00 a.m. on July 23, the *Big Hatchie* pushed off from the landing at Hermann. Suddenly, it was ripped by an explosion that decimated the forward cabin of the boat and poured steam throughout the main deck. The details are sketchy, but evidently, at least five crew members and cabin passengers were killed instantly. Of those who were identified, another seventeen were scalded, seven of them seriously. Captain Frisbee was standing on the hurricane deck at the time of the explosion. Despite being hurled over the pilothouse, he escaped injury. Many of the German deck passengers were killed, either scalded to death or blown into the river. Because the ship's books were destroyed in the blast, it was impossible to determine how many were killed in the accident.

The remains of the boat drifted two miles downriver, where it stayed until it was towed back to Hermann by the *Wapello*. The *Wapello* took some of the wounded to St. Louis. The *Big Hatchie* did not sink. It was apparently rebuilt, because *Way's Packet Directory* says it was sold to the U.S. government in 1846.

The newspapers were incensed by the disaster and called for an investigation to punish the responsible parties. Captain Frisbee was charged in federal court with misconduct and neglect under the Steamboat Act of 1838. At trial, the government tried to prove that Frisbee employed an incompetent engineer, Barry Mohan, who allowed too much steam into the boilers as the vessel was leaving the landing. However, the evidence showed that Mohan had built and repaired steam engines for several years and served on the river under one of the most respected engineers on the Mississippi. He was described as "steady, sober, industrious and careful." Several citizens of Memphis, Frisbee's hometown, sent a petition describing the captain as a skillful and cautious commander.

This obelisk commemorates the thirty-five German immigrants who died on the *Big Hatchie* and were buried in an unmarked grave. The disaster occurred in 1845, not 1842, as inscribed on the memorial. *Author photo.*

As for the cause of the disaster, an examination of the boiler that exploded revealed that it had an internal crack not visible from the outside that went nearly all the way around it. In some places, the crack was one-eighth of an inch deep. Captain Frisbee was acquitted.

The citizens of Hermann erected a memorial to thirty-five unidentified victims of the blast buried in a mass grave at the top of the hill in the town's cemetery. Curiously, the inscription gives the date of the explosion as 1842 instead of 1845. It still stands (although it was replaced by an identical marker in later years).

THE *TIMOUR*

The *Timour* was another of the "unlucky boats." After being badly damaged in the Great St. Louis Fire of 1849, it was rebuilt. On July 29, 1852, it hit a snag nine miles above Boonville, Missouri, and sank. The cargo it was carrying was badly damaged, but the boat was raised and repaired. The *Timour* sank again eight miles below Rocheport, Missouri, on December 5, 1853, when it hit a log and sustained damage to the hull. Again, the damage was slight enough to repair and for the ship to return to the river.

Ultimately, the *Timour* met with disaster that could not be repaired. It exploded on August 20, 1854 (some sources say September 25, 1854), at Edward's woodyard three miles below Jefferson City, Missouri. The three boilers on the boat exploded simultaneously, killing fifteen people, including the clerk, the bookkeeper, a fireman, the master and the pilot, Charles Dix. The pilot was thrown overboard by the force of the explosion and drowned. More people might have been killed or injured, but the passengers had taken advantage of the stop for wood to walk up a nearby hill. When the boilers blew, a safe joined them on that hillside.

THE *CATARACT*

The *Cataract*, on a journey between St. Louis and Kansas City in late November 1857, stopped for wood at Shippingsport, a few miles above Arrow Rock. It was night, and most passengers were asleep. As the steamboat resumed the journey, the mud receiver exploded, broke through the main deck into the hold below and went through the cabin floor and hurricane deck above. When hot steam filled the boat, it extinguished all the lights, leaving terrified passengers and crew to blindly try to escape danger.

Captain O'Neil took action by breaking the skylight in the cabin to allow steam to escape. He then rushed into the ladies' cabin and led the women and children to safety, resulting in no injuries among that group of passengers.

Others were not so fortunate. There were sixty-six passengers on board; thirty-nine were scalded, twenty-one badly. Fifteen passengers eventually died, three immediately. Nine of the most badly wounded were transported right away by the steamboat *Low Water* to Glasgow, Missouri, where another four died. The *Emma* retrieved the remaining passengers. As the *Emma* passed Glasgow, it reported an additional unknown number had died on board the destroyed *Cataract*.

The *Saluda*

These were terrible tragedies, but the worst came on Good Friday 1852, in the thriving western Missouri port of Lexington.

An Old Hulk of a Freight Boat

Captain Francis T. Belt was anxious to find cargo and passengers for his boat the *Saluda*. Belt was thirty-five years old and part of a river family. He and his brother Lloyd had an unfortunate experience when their vessel the *Planter* exploded on January 5, 1848, on the Illinois River while loading grain, killing five persons. Nonetheless, Belt was considered an "experienced boatman…[and] an able commander." Belt had just purchased a one-half interest in the *Saluda* from Peter Conrad for $1,200 in mid-March 1852. Nearly two weeks had passed, and the boat was still idled at St. Louis. Even though it was early in the season and the river was clogged with ice, Belt wanted to get his vessel underway. No steamboat made money sitting at the landing.

Eli Kelsey, an elder of the Church of Jesus Christ of Latter-day Saints—better known as the Mormons—was anxious as well. A total of 333 Mormons from England, Wales and Scotland had traveled from Liverpool to New Orleans, and from there to St. Louis on their way to Utah. Now Kelsey needed a boat to take them to Kanesville (near Council Bluffs), where they would join one of dozens of wagon trains headed west.

The "first class" boats were waiting for more favorable river conditions, not wanting to risk the trip up the icy and, even in normal conditions, treacherous Missouri. The *Saluda* was a good boat at one time; on one trip, its passengers inserted a card in the *Glasgow Times* commending it "as a safe, good boat and the Captain and crew as careful, vigilant and universally accommodating." Its hull was built in Cincinnati and towed to St. Louis to be completed. The boat was 179 feet long and 27 feet wide and was equipped with two boilers, two engines and two side wheels 20 feet in diameter. The *Saluda* made twenty-one trips between 1849 and 1851 up the Missouri River. At six years old, it had outlived the average Missouri River steamboat by three years, although most of one of those years was spent under water after it struck a snag and sank five miles south of Rocheport in central Missouri in 1847. Sand and silt accumulated around it, creating a new sandbar. A Boonville investor paid $800 for the hulk and had it raised and rebuilt in St. Louis. It was back on the river by February 1848. Conrad purchased it in 1851. By 1852, the *Saluda* was described as slow, underpowered and "an old hulk of a freight boat." It had two advantages that attracted Kelsey: its captain was willing to leave immediately, and the fare was cheap.

Belt agreed to take about 110 of Kelsey's immigrants. When the *Saluda* departed on March 30, there were 23 crew members and about 90 other passengers in addition to the Mormons. The vessel's officers in addition to Belt were Ferdinand Brockman, first clerk; Jonathan Blackburn, second clerk; Charles LaBarge, first pilot; Louis Guerette, second pilot; Josiah Clancy, engineer; and John Evans, engineer. Peter Conrad served as the bartender. Of the 38 known cabin passengers, 17 were traveling to the Kansas City area. The remainder were headed farther upriver, no doubt to join wagon trains headed west, just as the Mormons (almost all of whom were deck passengers) were.

Despite being old and slow, the *Saluda* made decent time up the Missouri. It reached Glasgow, about 250 miles from St. Louis, on April 2. The next day, the *Saluda* stopped at Brunswick (in 1852 still on the river) and dropped off about ten of the Mormons, who left to buy cattle and go overland to Kanesville. There was little to be seen from the boat—just drifting ice, trees, snags, the occasional sandbar and "muddy, unpleasant water." On Sunday, April 4, Lexington, some 340 miles from St. Louis, hove into view on a bluff on the south bank. Just ahead was one of the most treacherous parts of the river, the Lexington Bend. West of the town, the river took a nearly right-angle turn to the northwest. The current rushed around the bend, crossing from the north bank to the south bank with a force that required all the power a boat could muster to navigate it. The "easy water was close ashore and the current outside, and therefore [one] must hug the bank upstream." The *Saluda* was not yet up to the task. Henry Ballard, one of the Mormons on board, recorded in his diary the efforts to make it past the bend.

> *April 4, Sun. We reached Lexington, and the captain and the firemen did their best to make headway at this point, where it ran very swift, and after trying several hours they gave it up and crossed to the other side of the river, where there were no houses and tied up the boat for the night.*
>
> *April 5. The river was floating full of ice, large blocks from two feet thick and two rods long and larger. So we could not move any for four days.*
>
> *April 8, Thursday morning we crossed back to Lexington. The ice was not floating quite so bad. It broke the paddle wheels some and they repaired them for starting the next day.*

LAUNCHED INTO ETERNITY

Lexington, the third-largest town in Missouri at 2,700 residents and growing, sat on top of a bluff. It was a major commercial center and port on the Missouri River, shipping hemp (used to make rope for cotton bales), tobacco and other crops. At the foot of the bluff in an area known to the locals as "under the hill" were upper and lower steamboat landings and several log and brick warehouses. The town itself boasted a nearly new Greek Revival courthouse that would survive the Civil War, albeit with a cannonball embedded in one of its pillars (it survives today as well), as well as a Gothic church, a college and several businesses. Its citizens included William H. Russell, who, along with Alexander Majors and William Waddell, founded a successful freight company and, eight years later, the Pony Express.

As the *Saluda* lay at the upper landing, it was joined on April 8 at the lower landing by the *Isabel* under Captain William Miller. On board the *Isabel* was Abraham Smoot. Smoot was, like Eli Kelsey, arranging passages and buying supplies for Mormons headed up the river to join wagon trains to Utah. Kelsey had urged Smoot to go on the *Saluda*—Captain Belt even offered to take him for free—but Smoot declined. He took the *Isabel* instead a couple of days later.

The William Dunbar family, Mormons from Scotland, intended to board the *Saluda* at St. Louis but literally missed the boat by a few minutes waiting for their supplies to be delivered. They obtained passage on another boat with the understanding that the captain would transfer them to the *Saluda* when they caught up with it. However, neither boat was at the same landing at the same time, and the Dunbars ended up in St. Joseph, some 160 miles upstream. For reasons that were never explained, Dunbar insisted that the captain take his family back downriver to the *Saluda*. They arrived at Lexington on April 8, ready to embark the next day. Because the boiler deck was already crowded with Mormon immigrants, the Dunbars found refuge from the weather under a tarpaulin erected by the crew on the hurricane deck directly above the boilers.

Good Friday, April 9, 1852, dawned gray, cold and misty. The travelers were ready to leave Lexington. The passengers had huddled on the main deck for days, enduring a hard rain on Sunday and snow on Monday. A number of them decided to leave the boat and go overland to their destination. The exact number of those who left isn't known, but it probably included the cabin passengers who were going to Independence and Kansas City, just a few miles upstream. According to William G. Hartley and Fred E. Woods, about 175 passengers and a crew of 23 were on board that morning.

Early that morning, Captains Belt and Miller conferred about river conditions. Miller believed that the *Saluda* was too old and not up to the task of getting past the Lexington Bend when the river was running high and swift with ice floes in it. It was later reported—and disputed by Belt's family—that Captain Belt declared to Miller, "I will round that point this morning or blow this boat to hell!" Belt also conferred with his engineer, Josiah Clancy. Belt undoubtedly instructed Clancy to make as much steam as possible to enable the *Saluda* to make enough headway to traverse the bend. Whether he told Clancy to take measures that would endanger the boat is also disputed. Belt's family claimed that he was cautious and prudent nearly to the point of timidity. Others claimed that he dressed down Clancy for failing to provide sufficient power during the previous attempts and directed Clancy to make enough steam whatever the risks.

At 7:30 a.m., Captain Belt gave the order to cast off from the shore. He and the first clerk, Ferdinand Brockman, were talking on the hurricane deck between the chimneys. Second Clerk Jonathan Blackburn just left them for the ladies' cabins at the rear of the boiler deck. The pilots Charles LaBarge and Louis Guerette were in the pilothouse and rang the bell to signal that the *Saluda* was underway. The boat swung into the current, and ten crewmen were on the port afterguard using poles to push the stern away from the shore. A butcher who had just delivered supplies to the boat was on shore and let loose the lines. William Dunbar left his family eating breakfast on the hurricane deck to speak to a friend near the back of the boat. Henry Ballard was enjoying a morning cup of coffee. Matilda Wiseman, hired by John Sargent to be the governess for his two children, had agreed to marry him. She finished putting on her wedding dress for the ceremony to be performed later that morning. The forward main deck was crowded with passengers, there to watch the boat finally get underway and perhaps to gather some warmth from the fireboxes and boilers that were being stoked to make maximum steam.

Engineer Clancy let the water in the boilers grow low, and then he opened the valves to let the cold water from the river enter the red-hot boilers. Almost instantly, steam filled the boilers. The boat's paddle wheels made two or three revolutions.

Suddenly, Lexington was rocked by a tremendous explosion that rattled the homes and buildings on the bluff. The *Saluda* erupted into a cloud of steam, smoke, debris, bodies and body parts. George Gaunt saw LaBarge and Guerette hurled, along with the remains of the pilothouse, into the river. Their bodies would not be recovered. Captain Belt and First Clerk Brockman were thrown on shore. Colonel James Hale was watching the *Saluda* leave from the top of the bluff. He wrote about the horrific results of the explosion a few years later.

> *The current caught the wrecked boat and threw it back against the levee, where it was tied up, the bow resting against the shore, with the lower forward deck above the water and the stern several feet below the surface.*
>
> *As the writer ran down the hill the first thing he saw was the boat's safe lying in the road, back of what is now the waterworks power house. The safe was intact, and chained to it was a dead yellow spotted pointer dog. This was about seventy yards from where the explosion occurred.*
>
> *In the flat just west of the power house was the dead body of a large man, lying with his face downward and his limbs extended as if he had sailed through the air like a blue rock. Every thread of clothing had been blown off his body. A sheet was soon spread over him and he was identified as Captain Belt, commander of the boat.*

The explosion of the *Saluda* as depicted in this painting by Terry McKee. *Lafayette County Historical Society.*

The citizens of Lexington rushed down to the levee "under the hill" to rescue the survivors and to collect the dead. Some brought mattresses on which twenty-two horribly burned men, "their faces perfectly red from severe scalds," were placed. Twelve died within the hour from having inhaled steam. Another eleven were brought to a warehouse set up as a temporary hospital. Others were taken to private residences. William Dunbar, stunned by the blast and covered with blood, was taken to the warehouse, where he saw the bodies of his wife and daughter. His daughter was "so mangled," he later wrote, "that I could scarcely recognize her." And, indeed, another survivor claimed that the body was that of *her* daughter. Dunbar never saw the body again, and for the rest of his life he wondered if he had been mistaken and she had somehow survived. Matilda Wiseman was thrown into the river and rescued. John Sargent and one of his children were killed. Half-owner Peter Conrad was dangerously burned. Henry Ballard was blown into a bunk on the boat. To his horror, the man next to him had his brains blown out. Ballard lay there stunned for a half hour before he was able to stumble off the boat and collapse on the shore with a head wound of his own.

Others were trapped in the wreckage. Two-thirds of the boat was "a mass of ruins, beneath which were lying men, women and children; some of whom were yet alive. Their groans, shrieks and sobs, and the plaintive wailing of helpless babes carried grief and desolation to the hearts of those who were exerting themselves to relieve their suffers." On the levee lay "twenty-six mangled corpses collected together and as many more with limbs broken, and torn off, and bodies badly scalded."

Three citizen committees were quickly formed to care for the injured, to bury the dead and to collect money for the relief of the survivors. That night, twenty-one victims were buried in the Machpelah Cemetery in a trench dug in the potter's field. The "ladies of our city," the *Lexington Express* noted, "were active in affording relief to the wounded females, laying out the dead, and securing protection for the children who were saved." The exact number of persons killed in the explosion is unknown. Abraham Smoot estimated that about seventy-five died (twenty-eight of them Mormons) on that Good Friday, a number that historians Hartley and Woods concluded, after much research, was the best estimate.

Hearing of the disaster, Eli Kelsey rushed to Lexington to provide such assistance as he could. He tried to find out how many Mormons were killed, but many of the uninjured survivors had continued to Kanesville on the *Isabel*, having taken up Captain Miller's generous offer to provide them free passage to their destination.

Several children were left as orphans. Most continued the trip to Utah, but some remained behind and were adopted by Lexington residents. One family offered to pay for the Sargent children to return to England. They declined (or, more likely, someone declined for them). The younger ones were taken to Utah. The eldest, Ellen (age twelve), chose to remain in Missouri. She married in 1861 and died in 1868. Duncan Kelsey Campbell, the infant son of Duncan Campbell, was the only survivor of his family. He was taken in by Alexander McFadden. Later that year, he was declared Alexander's legal heir, and his name was changed to George C. McFadden. George became a printer and, unfortunately, acquired a reputation as a hail-fellow-well-met and a drinker. When Alexander died in 1882, he left George only $1.00 from his estate. George died in 1894 when he fell under the wheels of a Santa Fe Railroad freight train near Emporia, Kansas. The only other confirmed adoption was that of Mary Cramer, who went to live with Caspar Gruber. Gruber had other mementos of the *Saluda*. He bought its hull and removed oak timbers from it to build a house, which he occupied as late as 1898. A door from the boat Gruber used in his house is in the Lexington Historical Society Museum. The *Saluda*'s bell was salvaged and sold for $17.50 to a minister in Savannah, Missouri (a

The *Saluda*'s bell was recovered and sold to a minister in Savannah, Missouri. It now hangs in a memorial wall at the Savannah First Christian Church. *Author photo.*

The *Saluda* Memorial, erected in 2002 on the 150th anniversary of the disaster, stands across the street from the Lexington Historical Society Museum in Lexington, Missouri. *Author photo.*

few miles north of St. Joseph). It is today in a memorial wall in front of the Savannah First Christian Church.

The reaction to the disastrous explosion was immediate and strengthened calls for legislation to provide more regulation for steamboat operations. On April 4, the steamer *Glencoe*'s three boilers exploded while it was docked at St. Louis, killing forty or more persons. The *Glasgow Weekly Times* noted the *Glencoe* and *Saluda* explosions and lamented, "Within a few days of each other hundreds of persons have been suddenly launched into eternity without one moments warning….Is there no remedy for this wholesale destruction of life?"

Neither the Mormon Church nor the town forgot the victims of the *Saluda*. In 1991, the descendants of John Sargent erected a monument in Machpelah Cemetery to those who died. In 2002, as part of Lexington's commemoration of the 150th anniversary of the explosion, the Mormon Historic Sites Foundation established a park with plaques and a bell across the street from the Lexington Historical Society building.

5

FIRE AND ICE

Fearsome Fire

In 1849, the St. Louis levee was the epicenter of St. Louis life. New people arrived every day by steamer, either to make a new life in the city or as a stop on the way to a new life in the West. Tons of goods were loaded and unloaded. And it was the starting point for many a voyage up the Missouri River. This meant there was always a long line of steamboats tied up at the levee waiting to load, unload or start on their way. The levee was also the starting point on May 17, 1849, of the Great St. Louis Fire.

On the night of the fire, the night watchman for the steamboat *White Cloud* reported to work at 9:00 p.m. He met an unfamiliar man leaving the boat as he was coming on board. The watchman questioned the visitor, who said he was looking for a friend. The watchman accepted that answer and proceeded on his rounds, finding nothing out of the ordinary. Thirty minutes later, the watchman smelled smoke and found the ladies' cabin in flames. He sounded the fire bell.

Three volunteer fire companies responded and fought the fire, but it grew too quickly, spreading to the steamer *Edward Bates*, tied up alongside the *White Cloud*.

Either the fire burned through the ropes holding the *Bates* to the levee, or the crew untied the ropes, hoping it would float away from the burning *White Cloud*, but the result was to have the fully flaming steamboat spin out of control and hit the *Belle Isle* and *Julia*, cinders flying and spreading fire to their decks. The *Bates* continued on its fiery path of destruction, setting fire to the *Taglioni*, the *Boreas No. 3*, the *Alice*, the *American Eagle*, the *Sarah*, the *Montauk*, the *Kit Carson*, the *Timour*, the *Acadia*, the *Mameluke*, the *Prairie State*, the *St. Peters*, the *Red Wing*, the *Alexander Hamilton*, the *Martha*, the *Eliza Stewart*, the *Mandan*, the *General Brooks* and the *Frolic*. The *Edward Bates* finally ran aground on Duncan Island. However, the *White Cloud* by then had broken free of its moorings and set the *Eagle* on fire.

There were piles of freight on the levee, and the wind carried cinders toward the shore, setting on bales of hemp and piles of wood and setting them ablaze. Tragically barreled lard and bacon were also among the freight waiting to be transported. They burst into flames, turning the levee into a raging inferno.

Other volunteer fire companies arrived and fought the fire that had by now spread to buildings along the levee. The city burned block by block.

Residents and merchants rushed to escape and move personal goods and merchandise away from the spreading fire. Looters took advantage of

A lithograph of the Great St. Louis Fire of 1849 by Nathaniel Currier, dated 1849. There are no known photographs of this disaster. *Missouri Historical Society.*

conditions and grabbed anything they thought might be of value before it turned to ashes.

As the night wore on, water supplies were exhausted, as were the men fighting the great fire. The river was tapped for water in a last effort to extinguish the blaze.

A hard decision had to be made. The only way to stop the fire was to take away its fuel, and that meant blowing up buildings in the path of the fire, creating a firebreak. The only means of blowing up the buildings was to use barrels of gunpowder—place the barrels in the fire's path and run like hell before they exploded. There was no way to control when the gunpowder would explode. Although it resulted in the death of three men when one of the barrels of gunpowder exploded prematurely, the maneuver saved the city.

Total loss was estimated to be from $3.5 million to $6 million ($100 to $170 million in today's terms). That included 280 businesses, 430 buildings, 23 steamboats and an unknown number of lives, including the brave fire captain, Thomas Targee, who is credited with saving the city with his firebreak plan.

A definitive answer to the question of how the fire started has never been provided. One theory was that it was arson to collect insurance money for the *White Cloud*. Alternatively, an account by an eyewitness, part of the collection of the Missouri Historical Society, tells of an earlier fire that same day aboard the *White Cloud*. George Kyler heard the *White Cloud*'s fire bell and saw mattresses burning on the upper deck of the boat. Some of the mattresses were thrown overboard, and the rest were returned to the cabin. Could these have smoldered, eventually flaring up and causing the fire that started it all? And who was the unidentified man the watchman met on the steamboat earlier in the evening? What was his true business?

In the end, after an extensive investigation, no charges were brought. The origins of the Great St. Louis Fire remain shrouded in mystery.

Frozen Disaster

Ice gorges—ice floes that clogged the river and froze over—were familiar and dangerous events on the winter waters of the Missouri River.

In December 1865, an ice gorge formed along the St. Louis levee and did not clear until January 1866. The ice caused damage to many steamboats tied up there, including to the *Cora (No. 2)*, a favorite boat of Captain Joseph Kinney. Dr. E.B. Trail, a steamboat historian, wrote of the *Cora*:

> *The favorite of the many boats of Captain Kinney was his steamer* Cora *(No. 2). She was not only his favorite but his greatest money maker. During the summer he worked her in the Missouri River trade, and in the late fall he took her south and worked her during the winter in the packet trade on the southern rivers. Her master was Captain J.B. Kinney, the only son of Captain Joseph Kinney.*

It was during one of these moves south when the *Cora*, with the Kinney family aboard, stopped for Captain Kinney to take care of some last-minute business in St. Louis. The steamboat was named after one of Captain Joseph Kinney's daughters, and it is this same daughter who wrote to Dr. Trail about their experience during the ice gorge. The family was at the St. Louis levee on their way to New Orleans for the winter when they were delayed by the unexpected ice gorge. They were still aboard the *Cora*, preparing to move to a hotel, when the ice began to break up and boats drifted from the shore. Cora Kinney wrote, "[Captain Kinney called] '…get all your wraps and don't stop a minute to pack your trunks, as there is no time to lose.'"

While exiting, the stage plank was pulled out from under Mrs. Kinney's feet as the rope holding it broke and the *Cora* swung away from the dock. Captain J.B. Kinney stayed on board the boat and, with the help of a porter, managed to throw one trunk of their belongings onto the levee.

Cora described the scene on the levee:

> *That broad levee—as far as you could see, was a solid mass of people that resembled a huge swarm of bees more than anything I can think of. It sounded like everybody was screaming. And the boats whistling as many were being crushed like toys. We children were grabbed by some would-be helpers, but as we did not understand, we clung to mother and each other, thinking we were going to be carried off. There were many fights and much stealing to get what they could off the many boats.*

The family finally made it to safety off the levee and were transported to the Planter's Hotel, only to find it on fire! They continued to the Southern Hotel and remained for the winter.

A description of the finale of the ice gorge appeared in the *St. Louis Republican* on January 13, 1866, when it finally broke:

This photo shows steamboats trapped on the St. Louis levee during the ice gorge of December 1866–January 1867. From left, the steamboats are *Omaha, Geneva, Big Horn, Montana, Hattie May, Bannock City, Diadem, Cora* and *Highlander. State Historical Society of Missouri, Columbia, Missouri.*

The scene on the landing at nine o'clock a.m. was truly imposing and in many respects picturesque and beautiful. Small and large cliffs of ice were scattered here and there along the surface of the mighty river, and seemed to shake their silvery locks at the softening elements that had invaded their arctic domain. Glossy and shallow lakes of water glided smoothly over the surface of the ice below, upon which the sun gleamed with brilliancy and beauty.

The story called for the city to provide help in breaking up the gorges before damage occurred and to ring bells on boats to warn when the ice moved. And the ice moved several times during that day. At 10:30 p.m., the paper reported:

The mighty current was pressing resistlessly onward and carrying its frozen freight tumultuously upon its swelling bosom. The ice came down cracking, crashing, grating, rumbling with thundering vehemence. The timbers of the boats remaining…could be heard creaking and breaking.

Steamboat Disasters of the Lower Missouri River

The steamboat *John Trendley* is trapped in an ice gorge, possibly from 1887. The second boat is *Rescue No. 2*. Both were owned by the Wiggins Ferry Company. *Missouri Historical Society*.

By the time the ice gorge broke, it had caused $700,000 in damage.

The *Cora* (and Cora) survived that disaster, only for the steamboat to sink on a trip between Fort Benton, Montana Territory, and St. Louis in 1869. Captain Edward Baldwin was a young pilot serving under his father on the *Cora*. On August 13, 1869, the elder Baldwin left the *Cora* in the charge of his son so he could eat his noon meal. He instructed the young man to "run the bend" and under no circumstances enter the chute, as there was a very dangerous snag known to be present in that location. The pilot disobeyed his father in an effort to save time and tried to sneak through the chute. The *Cora* struck the snag and went to its grave. The wreckage caught so much sand and silt that it created the one-thousand-acre Cora Island, now a wildlife refuge.

Obviously, St. Louis was not the only place along the river that had to deal with ice gorges, but ice often moved downstream, making it worse there. With enough ice gorges forming on their own, it is disconcerting to find out that sometimes they were deliberately caused.

In 1888, an ice gorge in St. Louis was responsible for between $60,000 and $100,000 in damage. One of the captains of the Missouri Pacific ferryboats admitted they deliberately formed the gorge:

Cora Island, formed when the steamboat *Cora (No. 2)* sank, is located in St. Charles County, Missouri. *United States Forestry Service.*

> *Yes, we choked her up* [said Captain Charles Teller of the Missouri] *There was a channel about fifty yards wide and I went up with the Missouri and Captain Joe Teller took the Pacific and we laid broadside of the channel. That stopped the fine ice and as it was a cold night it soon closed the opening. We did it simply to protect ourselves. If the boats above us will not come down and keep this threat clear we will have to stop it up and let them take their chances.*

Another unnamed captain said, "If I can work my way through the ice and make $10,000 by it, but smash up another boat by starting the ice down on it, I have a right to do it. That is marine law."

On January 27, 1881, the *St. Louis Globe Democrat* described the situation as follows: "ice coming in large quantities through the narrow channels between the ice fields, and in order to keep the river open at that point they ran the two boats up into the channel and held the ice back until a gorge… was formed, and held all the floating ice until it filled the entire harbor.

The *Globe Democrat* reported that the Wiggins Ferry Company's *Rescue No. 2* (a tugboat) attempted to clear the gorge by cutting a canal through the gorge downstream, opening the channel to the lower end of the obstruction to give boats trapped by the ice a chance to escape danger before the gorge broke.

6
DISEASE DISASTERS

In 1832, when cholera made its first appearance in the United States, the disease grew to be more dreaded than smallpox, because there was no cure. Patients with smallpox had a chance to recover, and if they did, they would be immune. With cholera, there was no recovery and, at the time, no known cause. The patient initially fell ill with diarrhea and cramps, followed by vomiting. The resulting dehydration was the killer. The cause, as we know now, was contamination, such as sewage in the drinking water. Regrettably for those living along the Missouri River, steamboats often carried passengers who were sick with the disease right to their doors.

The famous steamboat captain Joseph LaBarge was traveling up the Missouri River in July 1833 on the steamboat *Yellowstone* when the crew was struck by cholera below Kansas City. The story, as LaBarge recounted it, was that everyone on board with the exception of himself and the boat's captain died of the disease. The captain, Andrew Bennett, left LaBarge in charge of the boat while he traveled back to St. Louis to hire a crew to finish their journey.

People in nearby Kansas City did not like the idea of a boat carrying cholera victims tied up nearby. A group of men approached the *Yellowstone* and, from a safe distance, threatened to burn it to the waterline if it was not moved from the vicinity immediately. LaBarge took their threats seriously and, on his own, fired up the boilers and steamed upstream to the west bank of the river.

Eventually, Captain Bennett returned with a new crew, and the *Yellowstone* continued its voyage.

Steamboat Disasters of the Lower Missouri River

The steamboat *Yellowstone* shown aground on a sandbar in the Missouri River in this painting by Karl Bodner, circa 1830s. *steamboattimes.org*.

LaBarge, during a later cholera outbreak in 1851, suffered additional losses due to the disease—fourteen passengers and crew—when he was captain of the *St. Ange*. When cholera victims died on board a boat, they were quickly buried along the shore in a shallow grave in plain wooden coffins built by the ship's carpenter. After a while, as the current ate at the bank of the river, a coffin might be uncovered and become visible to passersby. The riverbank could be pictured as a continuous graveyard.

Steamboats played a tragic role in the cholera epidemic that struck St. Louis in 1849. That year saw 4,285 deaths from the disease, according to the St. Louis Genealogical Society.

There were many contributing factors to the 1849 epidemic. The population was growing rapidly, and housing was scarce. This led to many people living together in one residence, often with an outhouse located near the well that provided drinking water. There was no sewer system, no stormwater management and only erratic trash collection in the city.

Where do steamboats fit into this picture? On January 2, 1849, two steamboats arrived in St. Louis with sixty-six passengers suffering from cholera. On January 6, the first St. Louisan died from the disease. It is believed the January 2 boat and its sick passengers were responsible for the initial outbreak. Steamboats brought a steady flow of new people into St. Louis, including many "49ers" on their way to California to find gold. The disease spread easily in the close confines of a steamboat and then continued to spread when someone who was sick or someone who left the boat not knowing they were sick entered the city's population.

As cholera deaths mounted in St. Louis, city officials sought a way to fight the disease. The Committee of Public Health was created on June 27. One of its first actions was to create a quarantine station for all steamboats headed for St. Louis, in the belief that stopping new cases of cholera from arriving would reduce the incidence of the disease.

All steamboats were required to stop at the quarantine station, and all passengers had to pass an inspection by a health officer. Initially, sick patients were quarantined on a steamboat hospital, but that soon proved inadequate. A hospital was hastily constructed on Arsenal Island (later known as Quarantine Island), south of the city. (Today, it is part of the eastern bank of the Mississippi River on the Illinois side.)

Steamboats were put on notice of the quarantine stop with a series of yellow flags flown on the *St. Louis*, the quarantine ship, and the yawls used by health officers. If a steamboat failed to stop, ten rounds were fired from a cannon to warn those upriver that diseased passengers might be headed their way. If the cannon failed to stop the boat, a messenger would be sent into the city to warn officials of the impending boat's arrival. Fire bells would sound an alarm, and police, firemen and citizens would prevent the steamboat from docking.

Other measures were also instituted to reduce the incidence of cholera. Standing water was drained, the keeping of hogs in the city was banned and streets and alleyways were paved.

By the end of July, the number of deaths was declining, and the worst of the epidemic was over.

Cholera-carrying steamboats were considered a threat to towns located along the Missouri River as well. Those river towns feared that steamboats carrying cholera would bring the disease and spread it among their citizens. The *James Monroe* set forth from St. Louis, heading upriver with a predominantly Mormon passenger list. Soon after they embarked, passengers began to fall ill. On approaching Jefferson City, Missouri, the fear among the citizenry was so great that the steamboat was not allowed to dock. A cannon on the bank of the river, coupled with the threat to blow the boat out of the water, stopped the *Monroe* a mile below the city.

STEAMBOAT DISASTERS OF THE LOWER MISSOURI RIVER

This engraving (date unknown) of Jefferson City, Missouri, shows the state capitol overlooking the Missouri River. *Library of Congress.*

Fear also ran rampant among passengers not yet ill with the disease. They left the boat and walked toward the city, many falling ill and dying along the way.

The citizens of Jefferson City eventually let compassion overcome fear. City churches turned into hospitals, and the stricken passengers were given care. The crew members who survived deserted the boat and left it abandoned for several months before it was returned to St. Louis.

Even when a boat was determined to be free of cholera, disaster could strike in another form. On May 28, 1850, after the cholera epidemic but with Quarantine Island still active, the steamboat *St. Louis* stopped, was inspected and its passengers given a clean bill of health. While the passengers were celebrating being sent on their way with little delay, the steamboat pulled away from the shore and headed toward the channel. With no warning, a boiler exploded. Seventeen to twenty people died in that explosion or by drowning when they tried to escape the boat. Another fifty-two were scalded, twenty-eight of them badly injured by the steam. The deaths and injuries were confined to deckhands and passengers on the lower deck, except for one extremely unlucky man, a Mr. Plummer, a cabin passenger. Plummer started down the stairs to the lower section of the boat at exactly the moment the explosion occurred, and he was badly mangled. Even worse, during the fear and confusion, his body was robbed of several thousand dollars by, as the *Western Watchman* newspaper described the individual, "a being…for whom our language furnishes no adequate term of execration."

And cholera was not the only disease carried by steamer up the Missouri River. In 1837, the *St. Peters* started up the river to deliver supplies to the American Fur Company at the mouth of the Yellowstone River. At the time, the *St. Peters* was the largest boat to ascend that far up the Missouri (2,200 miles).

Smallpox broke out among the deck crew before the boat reached St. Joseph, Missouri. Smallpox, as mentioned earlier, was not as feared as cholera, except by Native Americans, who had no immunity.

Runners went out to warn Native Americans to stay away from the river. According to Phil Chappell's *A History of the Missouri River*, the disease still reached tribes along the banks. The Mandans, with a population of 1,700 before the smallpox epidemic, numbered a paltry 31 after it broke. Within a year after the smallpox outbreak, the Pawnees had their population reduced by half, from 12,500 to 6,244.

7
CIVIL WAR

The Civil War initially disrupted much of the commerce on the Missouri River. Many boats were chartered or, in some cases, commandeered, to take soldiers and military supplies to Union troops in Tennessee and Arkansas and to bring the wounded and sick back to St. Louis. But events in the Northwest revived the Upper Missouri trade. The federal government needed men and materials for campaigns against Indian tribes who sought to take advantage of the distraction of the conflict between the states. Then, in 1862, John Bannock discovered gold in Grasshopper Creek in Montana Territory. Hundreds of men and women sought passage to the Upper Missouri to find their fortune. The steamboat business boomed again.

But boats had to contend with a new danger: Confederate guerrillas. To get to Montana Territory, the boats had to pass through Little Dixie—the counties bordering the river from Callaway County in mid-Missouri to Jackson County on the state's western border. Guerrilla bands fired into the boats as they passed. Sometimes, they briefly boarded the vessel to force its crew to take them from one side of the river to the other. And sometimes, when they boarded the boat, they took soldiers or former slaves off the boat to be executed. One such bloody incident occurred in 1863.

"WE WILL ONLY SHOOT THE BUCKS": THE ATTACK ON THE *NEW SAM GATY*

No doubt Eberhardt Schuttner was anxious to get home when he boarded the steamboat *New Sam Gaty* at Jefferson City. He and five fellow soldiers from Company E, Fifth Cavalry, Missouri State Militia—George Meyer, William Henry, Michael Tiess, George Schreiber and Henry Schweder—were to join the regiment at Independence and then travel to St. Joseph to be mustered out where they had been mustered into service barely one year before.

The Fifth Cavalry, recruited from the St. Joseph area, was commanded by Colonel William Penick. A staunch Unionist, Penick was to become one of the leading Radical Republicans in the state. His regiment reflected Penick's strong views. It had a large contingent of Germans who hated slaveholding secessionists and who, in turn, were hated by guerrillas. The Fifth Cavalry quickly became involved in an escalating round of depredations and summary executions—some of them especially gruesome—while fighting guerrillas in western Missouri.

Due to a cut in funding by Congress, in February 1863 the Missouri State Militia was reorganized. The initial plan was to transfer some of the companies en masse to their new regiment and to distribute the rest among existing companies. But in early March, new orders were issued. The Fifth Cavalry would be disbanded "in the interest of public service."

The regiment was ordered to assemble at Independence and then to go to St. Joseph to be mustered out of service. Most of Company E was going overland from Jefferson City and its other posts. But the horses belonging to Schuttner, Meyer, Henry, Tiess, Schreiber and Schweder were worn out. Their officers ordered them to take the steamboat *New Sam Gaty* instead. Henry was especially pleased to take the steamboat, because he had injured his back in a fall from his horse six months earlier and had not fully recovered. When the other men found out, they asked the "lucky" passengers to take their extra baggage, all of which was collected and piled into a government wagon box. Little did any of them know that the fortunate ones were those who were going to ride horses to Independence, not those on the steamboat.

A Boat "In First Rate Order…Perfectly Sound and Strong"

The *New Sam Gaty* was built in Louisville, Kentucky, in 1860. It was the *"New" Sam Gaty*, as there was already a boat named *Sam Gaty* operating on the Mississippi and Illinois Rivers between St. Louis and Peoria, Illinois. The boats were named after Samuel Gaty, a St. Louis industrialist who owned a foundry and machine shop that made parts for steamboat engines.

A side-wheeler, the *New Sam Gaty* was large for the Missouri River trade—367 tons. It was described as a "very plain boat," having originally been built as a freighter, with no Texas deck and only a short cabin on which the pilothouse sat to accommodate the crew. Although the *New Sam Gaty* was only three years old when it picked up the Fifth Cavalry soldiers at Jefferson City, it already had a checkered history.

After the boat was completed, the owner decided to make it suitable to haul passengers as well. This necessitated an inspection by officials of the U.S. Treasury Department. (The government inspected only passenger-carrying vessels under the federal laws then in effect.) The boat passed. However, on its shakedown cruise, near New Albany, Indiana, a boiler exploded, killing two men.

A subsequent investigation revealed that the builder had misrepresented the strength of its three boilers. They were rated for a pressure of 105 pounds per square inch, when they should have been rated at only 70 pounds per square inch. The investigators excused their failure to discover the fraud due to the fact that they saw the boat only after it was completed, with its fire brick masonry in place around the firebox and the boat's three boilers. The boat was repaired and entered service on the Missouri River out of St. Louis.

The war was not even a week old when the *New Sam Gaty* became embroiled in another controversy. On April 17, 1861, the boat was lying at Wayne City, the landing for Independence. In testimony at a later inquiry, Captain Thomas B. Johnson claimed that some "boys" brought a small secessionist flag on board and said that the boat should carry it. Someone, probably the second clerk, tied the flag to a pair of elk horns over the door to the boat's office, supposedly in sport. Johnson said he was afraid to take it down immediately, because he was in strong secessionist country. He ordered the mate to take it down after dark. But Johnson and the mate "forgot" about the flag (or so he said). When the *New Sam Gaty* arrived at the abolitionist and Union stronghold of Leavenworth the next day, the townsfolk spotted the secessionist flag flying from the boat. An immense, angry crowd gathered and demanded that the flag be taken down. Johnson hastened to remove it. Johnson was tried for his carelessness, but he was acquitted by a military commission in St. Louis. The suspicion that Johnson was a Southern sympathizer remained, and Union authorities later removed him from command of the vessel. For the next two years, the boat plied the Missouri River without any untoward incidents.

On the eve of its fateful voyage, the *Daily Missouri Republican* praised the *New Sam Gaty* as being "in first rate order; her hull is perfectly sound and strong, and she looks good for two or three years yet. She deserves the name *New Gaty*." Now under the command of Captain John McCloy, it was supposed to leave St. Louis bound for Leavenworth and Omaha on March 16, 1863. It was delayed by an unfortunate accident in which two of its crew members drowned in the Mississippi and did not embark until the late afternoon of March 17.

Its passengers included between ninety and one hundred "contrabands"—former slaves—who had been among the thousands of African Americans escaping to the post at Helena, Arkansas, almost as soon as Union troops occupied it. At the end of February, the Reverend Hugh Fisher, with the permission (and likely the encouragement) of Helena's commander, took about two hundred of them under his wing and saw to their transport to St. Louis. Fisher was no novice at helping escaped slaves to freedom. In 1861, while serving as a chaplain for one of James Lane's Kansas cavalry regiments, Fisher led a wagon train of former slaves out of southwest Missouri to freedom in Kansas.

Fisher did not intend for his flock to remain long in St. Louis. He put half on the *Magenta* and the rest on the *Gaty*, and the destination was Kansas. Fisher intended to go on the *Gaty* himself. "Just as the cable was cast and the last gang-plank was being drawn in," he later wrote, "I was impressed that I had better go via rail and prepare for the reception of the party." He sent an assistant, William Wilson, to take charge of the former slaves on board.

The trip was delayed when the boat's cylinder heads were damaged near Hermann three days after it left St. Louis. At first, the plan was to tow it back to the city. It apparently drifted downstream several miles, all the way to South Point (between Washington and Augusta), but its return to St. Louis was scrapped when arrangements were made to ship new cylinder heads by rail. They were installed, and by March 23, the *New Sam Gaty* resumed its trip upstream.

"Blow Their Brains Out!"

It was about eleven o'clock on the evening of March 27 when Schuttner and his fellow soldiers bedded down on the deck next to the wagon boxes of government supplies. It was a cool night on the river, and Schuttner had pulled a blanket over himself. His sleep was interrupted a couple of hours later by a harsh voice demanding, "Whose gun is this?"

Schuttner had left his Enfield rifle inside the wagon box next to him. He rose, still groggy. "That's my gun," he said to the figure in the dark. The man cursed and grabbed Schuttner's rifle. "Get up and get off the boat," he ordered. Schuttner, realizing that the boat had been captured by guerrillas, complied.

With the river running only about three and one-half feet, the pilot had taken the *New Sam Gaty* close to the south bank near Sibley, only thirty feet from a bluff. The guerrillas had been tracking the boat for some time. Their original plan was to board it at Napoleon, about ten miles downstream, but the boat did not land there. From atop the bluff, the guerrillas had the perfect spot to fire down on the boat and its crew if they failed to heed their warnings. And, indeed, both Sibley and Napoleon were favorite spots for guerrillas to ambush steamboats.

Schuttner was joined on shore by George Meyer and William Henry. Tiess and Schweder hid on the boat and were not discovered by the guerrillas. The mate claimed that George Schreiber was one of the deckhands, and he was not brought ashore. A couple of soldiers from the First Cavalry, Missouri State Militia, were on board, but they were left alone, because bushwhackers considered the men from that regiment to be "gentlemen," unlike Penick and the hated Fifth Cavalry. The guerrillas searched the men, taking $200 from Schuttner. The three men stood on the bank for nearly an hour, guarded by three raiders on horseback. While they waited in the cold night, other guerrillas searched the boat. They rifled through each passenger's belongings, taking money and jewelry ($450 from one man and $1,060 and a gold watch from another). The men broke into the boat's safe and stole $600.

Captain McCloy had been asleep as well. The guerrillas awakened him at gunpoint. Someone had tipped them off that the "Parson Fisher" was on board with a couple of hundred "contrabands." The bushwhackers threatened to burn the boat if Fisher was not produced, but the crew said the contrabands were in the charge of a soldier who could not be found. Warned by the crew, Wilson threw his Union officer's coat overboard and hid under a pile of castings.

Confederate guerrillas attacking a steamboat. From the *London Illustrated News*. *Missouri Historical Society*.

How the guerrillas knew about Fisher and the former slaves on board is a matter of conjecture. Patrick Riley, a steward on the *New Sam Gaty*, was arrested the following year in connection with another, less deadly, guerrilla attack on the *Prairie Rose*. Riley was fingered as "the man through whose instrumentality the *Gaty* was taken." Riley and another suspected Southern sympathizer were sent to St. Louis in chains for trial. Both, however, were later acquitted. On the other hand, Fisher (who went ahead of the boat) told the provost marshal at Leavenworth (who apparently told the newspapers) that 175 "contrabands" were on steamboats on their way from St. Louis. Perhaps Fisher had told others while traveling through Missouri. And certainly, the embarkation of 200 former slaves on steamboats bound for Kansas was hardly a secret in St. Louis.

The guerrillas ordered the African Americans off the boat. When Captain McCloy asked William Gregg, the guerrilla leader, what he intended to do with them, Gregg replied, "Blow their brains out!" McCloy begged him not to kill the former slaves. Finally, Gregg promised to shoot only "the bucks."

The attackers lined up about twenty black men on the shore along with the soldiers. The rest of the former slaves were assembled on shore nearby. One of the guerrillas went down the line of men, holding a lantern shoulder-high behind them. The guerrillas proceeded to shoot them in the head, killing six or perhaps nine of them (the accounts vary). The rest, along with the remaining black women and children, fled in terror into the night with the sound of the passengers' screams in their ears.

At the same time, other bushwhackers turned their attention to the soldiers. Meyer protested that he was with the First Cavalry, but a Southern sympathizer on the boat said Meyer was lying and that he was "a Penick man." The guerrillas shot him in the back. He died instantly.

Faced with certain death, Schuttner and Henry decided to make a break for safety. It was either that or be gunned down like Meyer. The boat had pulled over next to a wood lot that supplied fuel to passing vessels. There was a sawmill nearby. Schuttner ran to it as fast as he could, seeking cover. A bullet from one of the guerrillas' revolvers struck his hip and went all the way through. Driven by adrenaline and desperation, Schuttner kept running for the sawmill. The guerrillas rode after him in the dark.

Rods braced the chimney of the mill. To get to Schuttner, the bushwhackers had to duck under them and then ride around a pile of lumber stacked nearby. They kept firing, but it was too dark to see him. Schuttner's foot got stuck in some loose lumber, and he stumbled against the saw, cutting his shin about halfway between his knee and ankle.

Schuttner, now suffering from both the gunshot wound and the deep cut on his leg, managed to get to a thicket of hazel and sumac about seventy-five yards beyond the mill. The guerrillas came after him on horses, "surrounded the thicket, and whooped around, but there were some old logs there." He crawled under one of the logs, covered himself with leaves and lay still. After further hunting through the thicket, the guerrillas finally gave up.

Before Henry disappeared into the darkness, one of the guerrillas' shots went high and clipped the back of his head. He lay there bleeding profusely from a scalp wound, either stunned or feigning death. The witnesses from the boat thought he was killed. It was, however, only a graze and not the most serious injury he received that night. His injured back forgotten, Henry, too, got away from the attackers. But while escaping, he stumbled in the dark, fell and severely injured his right wrist.

The guerrillas returned to the *New Sam Gaty*. They spent the remaining time—possibly another hour or two—throwing government wagon boxes filled with supplies and sacks of flour and rice overboard. Their bloody work done, the bushwhackers disappeared into the night. The *New Sam Gaty* finally pushed off from the bank. Despite guerrilla demands that it return to St. Louis, Captain McCloy continued upstream to report the attack to Union authorities.

"Visit the Perpetrators with Death and Destruction"

The *New Sam Gaty* arrived at Independence the next day. Colonel Penick fired off a telegram to district headquarters in Jefferson City, reporting the deaths of Meyers and Henry and that twenty of the former slaves had been killed. District commander Benjamin Loan forwarded a copy of Penick's wire to the commanding general in Missouri, Major General Samuel Curtis. Loan penned a fiery letter to Curtis, saying, "There can no longer be any question but that the contest for the Supremacy in this State must be made a war of extermination." Curtis in turn sent both communications to Washington with his endorsement that seconded Loan's sentiment: "I have directed the general to visit the perpetrators with death and destruction if he can catch them. They deserve summary punishment, and I hope they will have it meted out to them."

Union newspapers reacted just as strongly. The *St. Joseph Morning Herald* condemned the raiders as "cowardly butchers" and perpetrators of "revolting act[s]." The *Daily Missouri Republican* recounted the basic facts and then sarcastically observed: "And this is civilized warfare! The gallant exploit is chuckled over by rebel sympathizers in St. Louis, who manufacture coarse jokes about the excessively amusing circumstance of the 'emancipation' of a number of contrabands!"

Both Schuttner and Henry survived. Schuttner found his way to a farmhouse after daybreak. There, he got civilian clothes (perhaps to disguise himself if he ran into more guerrillas) and a horse. He rode to Independence and reported to Colonel Penick. Henry was thought to have been killed, because the passengers and crew witnessed his being shot in the head. His brains were not "blown out," as reported in the press; it was only a glancing blow. His more serious problems were a months-old back injury and the damage to his wrist.

The regiment had not yet concentrated at Independence for muster out, and its surgeon was not present. Schuttner and Henry were treated by a civilian—a "citizen barber," according to Schuttner. The doctor (or barber) "ran an iron through the place in [Schuttner's] hip; and bandaged [his] leg," where the sawtooth had apparently cut through to the bone. He went home to recuperate and later rejoined the regiment in time to be mustered out in St. Joseph. Although hobbled by a bad back, a painful wrist and a scalp wound, Henry's injuries were thought at the time not to be serious, and he apparently remained with the regiment at Independence.

Both Schuttner and Henry sought pensions based on disabilities they suffered during their military service. Curiously, neither claimed that the gunshot wounds were the cause of their permanent injuries. Schuttner sought a pension for the injury to his leg when he fell into the buzz saw blade at Sibley. Henry sought a pension based on his back injury, not the wound to his head.

By April 25, all except eleven of the former slaves Fisher brought from Arkansas on the *New Sam Gaty* were accounted for. Two straggled into Independence a few days later. At least two of the missing—we do not know which two, only that they were a woman and a boy—were captured by guerrillas and sold back into slavery. The fate of the others—whether dead, captured or escaped—is not recorded. As with most African Americans' lives and deaths during this period, the details are lost to history.

Neither of the *Gatys* survived long after the war. The *Sam Gaty* struck a snag in the Mississippi River in 1866 and sank. The *New Sam Gaty* continued to transport Federal troops and supplies on the Missouri River until the end of the war. It operated on the river until, while down bound near Arrow Rock on June 27, 1868, the boat "took a sheer on the pilot, hit the shore where a projecting log listed her, shifted the boilers [and] set the boat afire." It was destroyed.

THE SUMMER OF 1864

By 1864, guerrilla attacks on steamboat traffic were so prevalent that captains had iron plates placed around the pilothouses to guard against gunfire. Union soldiers were detailed to ride the boats to prevent their capture. The river port of Rocheport became the headquarters of the notorious guerrilla "Bloody" Bill Anderson in the late summer. Steamboat captains risked grounding to avoid the hail of bullets from there when they passed. Instead of mooring on the riverbank at night, captains took to tying up in the middle of the river. A new threat emerged when General Sterling Price led an army of twelve thousand men into Missouri in September 1864.

THE *BRIGHT STAR*

The *Bright Star* came into service as a center-wheel steam ferryboat in Washington, Missouri, in 1864. The ferry was used to move citizens of Washington to safety from threat of attack by the Confederate army, a last effort to invade Missouri that frequently degenerated into a campaign of plunder and looting of civilians. On October 1, the ferry, captained by Frank Hoelscher with Robert Roehrig as engineer, carried soldiers and civilians to Warren County on the north bank of the river. Judge W. Owens, in command of the local militia, ordered the boat's captain to not let the *Bright Star* fall into enemy hands.

    On October 2, the *Bright Star* left Washington loaded with soldiers, some civilians and a cargo of government supplies and stores headed downriver for St. Charles, Missouri. General Sterling Price's men were camped at a place known as South Point, overlooking the river. Although the channel ran along the bluff directly under the campsite, the pilot decided the *Bright*

The steam ferry *Bright Star* functioned mostly as a ferry, but sometimes it carried freight from one point in Missouri to another in the state. The *Bright Star* did not have its hull or its boiler inspected by federal officials, because it operated solely in-state. A decision in a court case challenging the lack of inspection declared that Congress had no control over commerce strictly internal to a state. *State Historical Society of Missouri, Columbia, Missouri.*

Star would be safer from possible Confederate gunfire if it traveled on the shallower north side of the river.

As the ferry passed along the campsite, it ran aground. Immediately, the boat took small-arms fire. The captain ordered the cargo thrown overboard to lighten the load, and the *Bright Star* drifted free, continuing its successful escape to St. Charles.

In the meantime, Washington was left open, and General John Clark took the town uncontested. Rebel soldiers plundered and burned the railroad depot before searching the town for food, forage and usable horses. They took the latter and whatever else they wanted. After reports of Federal troops landing upriver, the Rebels left Washington in the late afternoon, taking with them the spoils they had collected.

THE *WEST WIND*

The steamboat *West Wind* was not so fortunate during the same campaign later in October 1864. Union forces led by Colonel Chester Harding left St. Joseph on October 5, 1864, on the *West Wind*. He was responding to a call for help to defend against a possible threat to Jefferson City by Price.

At Fort Leavenworth, Kansas, the *West Wind* joined up with the steamboat *Benton*. Their mission was to remove supplies from Lexington, Missouri, before the Rebels could capture them. Fearful of running into fire from the shore, the pilothouses were barricaded, and breastworks of cordwood surrounded the boilers. Progress was slow, because the river was low and the boats kept running aground. Cambridge, Missouri, was a nest of Confederate and guerrilla forces, but both boats passed by safely, scattering the Rebels by firing at them. They reached Glasgow, Missouri, on October 13. The *Benton*, being of shallower draft, unloaded its cargo and began the return trip to Leavenworth. The *West Wind* stayed behind.

Meanwhile, General Price had received word that there was a generous cache of small arms being stored in Glasgow's city hall. To obtain these arms, he ordered Colonel Sidney D. Jackman to take five hundred men, join with General John Clark, cross the river at Arrow Rock, Missouri, and march twenty miles up the east bank to Glasgow. General Joe Shelby would attack the town from the west bank. On October 15, Shelby commenced firing into the town, but Jackman's men approaching on the east bank did not arrive until two hours later. Shelby sent a skiff of volunteers to capture the *West Wind* so he could use the vessel to ferry his men across the river. They gained the boat under a hail of gunfire but found that the crew had disabled the engines.

The Federal troops had no artillery and fewer men. They retreated, but not before Harding ordered all public property destroyed. (In 1952, a bill was introduced in Congress to pay Glasgow $11,200 in compensation for the burning of city hall as ordered by a Federal officer.) The city hall was ruined, and the cache of arms was burned. Colonel Harding surrendered at 1:30 p.m.

Unfortunately, the stores removed from Lexington for safety were captured by Rebel forces. The Rebel victory meant fresh supplies for the Confederates and destruction for the town of Glasgow. While Rebel troops gained 1,200 small arms, 1,200 overcoats, 150 horses and a steamboat, the town lost 15 dwellings and the Presbyterian church, not to mention the loss of life on both sides. The Rebels burned the *West Wind*, took their spoils and left town.

The remains of the *West Wind* rested on the bottom of the Missouri River until World War II. At a time when scrap iron was in demand, the Army Corps of Engineers dug a two-ton engine from the riverbed. Old-timers in the area claimed it was from the *West Wind*.

THE *MARS*

The steamer *Mars* had a varied Civil War record on the Missouri and Mississippi Rivers, at times under the control of Federal troops and at other times under Confederate control. It was captured by Rebels at Helena, Arkansas, in May 1861 and retaken by Federal troops in 1863. In September 1864, on the Missouri River, the *Mars* was attacked by guerrillas at Rocheport. The crew of the *Mars* killed one guerrilla and wounded another before returning to Jefferson City for troops.

On May 19, 1865, the *Mars* carried five companies of the Fourth U.S. Volunteers upriver to serve in the North Western Indian Expedition. All the men were former Confederate prisoners of war who were given a choice: take a loyalty oath and enlist in the Union army to serve on the western frontier fighting Indians, or remain in prison. Those who chose the former to escape the dire conditions of confinement were known as "Galvanized Yankees."

Soon after, the steamboat *Mars* met with ultimate disaster, not at war with anything. The boat ran into a snag at Cogswell Landing, opposite the mouth of the Fishing River, and sank.

8
MURDERS, REVENGE, LYNCHING AND ILL-TREATMENT

Crime also rode aboard steamboats, often committed by the crew, one member against another.

THE *GENERAL MEADE*

In May 1882, the *General Meade* had an eventful journey upriver. One of the crew became ill with an unnamed disease and was put ashore. A woman passenger on the way to recover the body of her dead child died and was buried on the riverbank. Between these occurrences, two of the "colored [sic] roustabouts" fought, and one sliced the other's neck with a razor causing his death. The "negro [sic] crew" tied the murderer to a stanchion and intended to hang him as soon as it grew dark. The officers and other crew were unable to stop the lynching, and although the news report was not certain, "it is thought the fellow paid the penalty of his crime."

THE *J.M. CLENDENIN*

This incident on the *J.M. Clendenin* is less a crime story and more an example of the poor and unfair treatment of African Americans working on steamboats. In October 1853, an African American sister and brother were employed on the *Clendenin* as chambermaid and steward, respectively.

Steamboat Disasters of the Lower Missouri River

The *General Meade* suffered its final disaster on September 14, 1888, when it was sunk by a snag on Pelican Bar, better known as the "Missouri River Graveyard." *State Historical Society of Missouri, Columbia, Missouri.*

Both were freedmen. When the steamer docked at Jefferson City, Missouri, the chambermaid helped a lady passenger with her luggage, but a bandbox was accidentally left behind. When the maid refused to return to look for it, the passenger complained to the clerk of the boat. The clerk went searching for the chambermaid, and when he found her, in an effort to compel her to help the lady, pushed her. The steward was nearby and, seeing his sister being pushed, rushed to her defense and threatened the clerk with a glass tumbler. The men fought, and the steward struck the clerk with the tumbler, cutting his head open. The amount of blood excited the passengers, and they insisted the steward be whipped. The man was being led to the bow to be tied to the capstan preparatory to receiving his punishment when he broke away and dived into the water. He sank, passed under the boat and came up once. Before he could be rescued, the man drowned.

As an aside, Missouri governor (and future Confederate general) Sterling Price was a passenger on the *Clendenin* at the time.

Soon after this incident, on November 1, 1853, the *J.M. Clendenin* was snagged and sank near Bates Woodyard, about ten miles below Hermann, Missouri. The owner of that woodyard recovered the boat and created a saloon out of the cabin in nearby Berger, Missouri.

THE *JUDITH*

On its final, fatal voyage in July 1888, the steamboat *Judith* had a bloody trip.

The mate, James McDonough, had a problem with one of the African American deckhands, Ed Neil, and slapped him. The mate proceeded to work, thinking that was the end of the incident. The deckhand waited until later in the evening, when the mate's back was turned, and struck him a mortal blow on the back of the head. The murderer escaped into the woods.

That was not the end of the bloodshed on that voyage. Two crew members, John Anderson, a deckhand, and Jim Walker, the underboss of the deckhands, both African American, fought with axe and knife. Both were mightily injured, but neither died. They were arrested.

As the *Judith* steamed toward St. Louis, it struck a snag about twelve miles above the mouth of the Missouri River. The boat broke in two and sank in five minutes. Fortunately, no lives were lost. A nearby farmer opened his home to the passengers and crew. They spent the night there until a boat arrived to carry them to St. Louis.

THE *LADY LEE*

In July 1881, Antoine Valle, the captain of the night watch, and Emmett Jones, a roustabout, quarreled aboard the *Lady Lee*. Valle beat Jones about the head with a piece of wood until he was unconscious, nearly severing his ear. At that point, the injured man was thrown aboard the steamer *Fanny Lewis* with no care given to his wounds. Jones, after recovering, followed Valle to St. Louis and shot him in the head while he slept.

Jones initially escaped but was captured a few days later, tried and sentenced to be hanged.

In January 1884, Governor Thomas Crittenden commuted Jones's sentence to life in prison, reasoning, "He was brutally and inhumanly abused and beaten by one Antoine Valle…but to my mind there are some circumstances surrounding the case of which the courts could take no cognizance which should mitigate."

A second murder was committed in August 1881 aboard the *Lady Lee*. The victim held the same job as had Antoine Valle and was killed in the same manner. Charlie Reeves, the victim, was, according to the news report, "considered dangerous." During breakfast on the fateful day, he and George

Lewis, "a hard character," quarreled. Lewis drew his revolver while still at the table and shot Reeves in the left temple. As Reeves died, Lewis continued to eat his meal. Lewis was told he would be arrested in Boonville, Missouri, when the boat docked. Lewis remarked he would not be taken, jumped off the boat and sank. No attempt was made to rescue the murderer, and he was not seen again.

Early the next year, as the steamboat *Lady Lee* backed out of the landing at Sibley, Missouri, during a heavy wind, it hit a snag and sank.

THE *MATTIE BELL*

The *Mattie Bell* was another steamboat seemingly cursed by violence that came to a disastrous end.

In December 1879, three roustabouts on the steamer, John Bruno, James Sullivan and Pat Bowen, fought. Bruno knocked Sullivan into the river, and in return, Bowen struck Bruno and stunned him, then knocked him overboard. Sullivan was rescued, but Bruno drowned. Bowen was charged with murder.

On August 6, 1881, Phineas Silby, the first mate of the *Mattie Bell*, was stabbed at Rocheport by an unidentified black deckhand and died. The deckhand was arrested.

And in a stunning display of lack of care and attention to crew members' well-being, eight black roustabouts from the *Mattie Bell* were made to work out of doors for two days during a blizzard (probably cutting wood for the boiler). Their hands, feet and faces were badly frozen; four of the men had to have their hands and feet amputated at the Marine Hospital in St. Louis.

The *Mattie Bell* finally met its demise on January 31, 1888, when it was crushed in an ice gorge in St. Louis.

THE *BENTON* (NO. 2)

On the evening of September 9, 1890, a group of black deckhands on the *Benton (No. 2)* was shooting craps as the boat approached the mouth of the Missouri River. Nelson Dwyer claimed that Frank Lee was cheating. After exchanging blows with Lee and getting the worst of it, Dwyer went to the

A Benton (No. 2) deckhand was murdered at the mouth of the Missouri River. The authorities had to sort out whether the killing occurred in Missouri or Illinois. Washington Missouri Historical Society.

hold. He emerged with a gun and began firing. Instead of shooting Lee, however, he shot Sam Johnston in the abdomen. Dwyer ran to the bow of the boat. The other deckhands gave Johnston a revolver. Johnston rushed to the bow of the boat, shot Dwyer in the arm and collapsed. Dwyer and another man jumped into the river and swam to the shore. At first, there were conflicting stories about the identity of Johnston's assailants. The men from the boat said they were two black roustabouts; some "loiterers on the Levee" claimed Johnston was shot by two white men. Once the stories were untangled, the authorities put out a warrant for Dwyer's arrest.

But the identity of the killer wasn't the most difficult issue. Where was Johnston murdered? Missouri or Illinois? The police referred the case to federal prosecutors, who declined to investigate or press charges, because the federal courts had jurisdiction only over murders on the high seas. After interviewing the *Benton*'s entire crew, the police determined that Johnston was shot on the Missouri side of the river. That still didn't decide the matter. Was Johnston shot in St. Louis County or St. Charles County? It isn't clear from available records whether Dwyer was ever caught, but if he was, prosecutors finally decided that he would be tried in St. Louis County.

9
THE UNEASY RELATIONSHIP BETWEEN BRIDGES AND STEAMBOATS

The extension of the railroads into the areas served by steamboats introduced a new hazard: railroad bridges. By the turn of the twentieth century, there were twenty railroad bridges crossing the Lower Missouri River. The bridges were located where they best served the needs of the railroad and with little thought given to their effect on river navigation. It became necessary for steamboat chimneys to be hinged so that they could be lowered when passing under a bridge. The bridges were poorly lit and difficult to see in fog, on a rainy night or at other times of low visibility. Bridges also created dangerous eddies and whirlpools that could suck a boat into their piers or slam it against the shore.

The Wabash Bridge at St. Charles, Missouri, was particularly troublesome. Captain William Heckman condemned this bridge as a "menace to navigation [that] should never have been built in the shape and place it is located." A new bridge was built about two hundred yards downstream in 1936 and the old one removed, but not before two disasters occurred.

THE *ST. LUKE*

The *St. Luke* had two early distinctions until it earned a dubious third one. It was nicknamed the "Yellow Hammer," because it was painted yellow.

It also was the only steamer to make two round trips a week between St. Louis and Jefferson City.

At ten o'clock in the evening on May 2, 1875, the *St. Luke*, captained by George Keith, in attempting to pass between the piers of the Wabash Railroad bridge at St. Charles during very high water, struck one of the piers and was wrecked. The following account was published in the *St. Louis Post-Dispatch* the next day:

> *The night was very dark and the river full. Captain Townsend* [pilot] *was at the wheel, and endeavoring to make the bridge, struck a pier on the larboard side, tearing out the whole broadside of the boat, including part of the engine and machinery. The boat hugged the pier for a couple of minutes, and then, caught by the current, swung around and went down the river, rolling and pitching frightfully. Six persons went overboard at the first crash, and were lost. The passengers sprang from their berths and ran hither and thither—panic-stricken, and the scene was one of utmost confusion and greatest terror.*

An attempt was made to remove the passengers by lifeboat, eight at a time. Before the lifeboat could return from its first trip to shore, the *St. Luke* sank two miles below the bridge in fifteen feet of water up to the hurricane deck. The rest of the crew and passengers climbed to the hurricane roof and pilothouse, where they remained until removed by ferry after daylight.

Lost in the wreck were the deck sweeper, Tom Donnelly (originally reported as lost but turned up alive); a male passenger, unidentified; fireman William Brooks; and deck passengers Mary Dinan and her two daughters, Mary Jane and Margaret (ages nine and seven, respectively).

James Dinan, the husband and father of three of the drowned, gave his account of what happened to him and his family to a *St. Louis Post-Dispatch* reporter the next morning:

> *When the boat was sinking I was standing by the bulwark with my little son Thomas in my arms ready to go in the boats. Edward* [a second son] *was by my side and my wife and two daughters were behind me.*
>
> *The water was rushing in with great violence and my boy was swept from my arms, and myself washed overboard. When I arose to the surface...I clutched at a raft which was floating near me and got on it....* [I] *was whirled along at a terrible rate, for there was a very strong current. About*

three o'clock this morning the log drifted into an eddy underneath a high bluff. I saw some roots growing out of the bank and jumped at and caught them....I was saved....The place I got ashore is about ten miles this side of where the accident occurred....[A]fter eating I started for the place of the accident. When I arrived there, I found my two boys, but my wife and two girls—they were gone. Better for me, if I had been drowned likewise.

At that Mr. Dinan wept.

The Dinan family had lived in Kansas City, Missouri, where James Dinan, a native of Ireland, had worked for the Missouri-Kansas-Texas Railroad for the prior four years. He thought he could improve his condition with a better job in St. Louis, so he packed up his family, his possessions and his $305 in life savings and booked passage on the *St. Luke*. His wife, his daughters, his possessions and his savings were all lost when the boat sank.

Two years later, Dinan sued the Missouri River Packet Company, owner of the *St. Luke*, for damages for the loss of his wife and daughters. He was awarded $15,000 in a jury trial.

The Behemoth and the Bullet That Killed Wild Bill: The *Montana*

The *Montana* was, as historian William Lass termed it, a "behemoth" of steamboats that operated on the Missouri River. It was 252 feet long, with its stern paddle wheel adding another 30 feet to its length, The vessel was 48 feet, 8 inches wide, with guards along its hull that made its total width 58 feet. The *Montana* had four decks—a main deck, a boiler deck, a hurricane deck and a Texas deck—topped by a pilothouse that towered 50 feet over the river. It could accommodate one hundred passengers, who could enjoy "custom-made upholstered furniture, expensive silverware, a piano." The *Montana* was 100 feet longer than most of the Missouri River boats. And yet, even with a full load of cargo and passengers, it drew only 3 feet of water.

The *Montana* and its sister boats, the *Wyoming* and *Dacotah*, were built by the Missouri River Transportation Company in 1878–79 at Pittsburgh. The company, better known as the Coulson Line for its owners Sanford, John, Martin and William Coulson, specialized (as its name implied) in freight business between St. Louis and Fort Benton, Montana (the head of

Steamboat Disasters of the Lower Missouri River

The *Montana* towers over the *Penguin* (foreground) at St. Charles, Missouri. The railroad bridge struck by the *Montana* can be seen in the background. *State Historical Society of Missouri, Columbia, Missouri.*

navigation on the Missouri River). The Coulsons hired or partnered with the best river pilots, among them Grant Marsh.

The Coulson Line was backed by eastern financiers, including William S. Evans. Evans was noted for wearing a diamond-studded pin and for his superstitious ways. Every boat the line owned had exactly seven letters in its name, because Evans believed that number brought good luck. His luck ran out when it came to the *Montana*. In May and June 1879, it made its only runs to Fort Benton (the first directly from Pittsburgh when its construction was completed), delivering 550 and 600 tons of cargo, respectively. On its second return trip, it was docked at Bismarck, North Dakota, on June 30, 1879, when a tornado ripped half of the cabin off the vessel and blew the cabin ashore. It cost $15,000 to repair the boat—nearly one-third of the original cost to build it. It never returned to its namesake state after that, being limited to carrying freight and passengers on the Mississippi and Lower Missouri Rivers.

The *Montana*'s luck did not improve with the years. In early May 1884, someone robbed the vessel's safe of $1,500 while it was docked at the St. Louis wharf. Its mate, Philip Schneider, was accused, but there was insufficient proof to charge him. Schneider remained with the boat. There was no trouble going upbound, but Captain George Keith insisted on stopping at Lexington, where he went ashore for about twenty minutes. Coming down bound, Keith stopped the boat at Kansas City, ostensibly to take on two passengers. But the passengers were no-shows. The delay prevented the *Montana* from making Lexington before dark. Keith landed the boat a few miles above Lexington to take on wood. Schneider was awakened by three masked men armed with revolvers. Schneider believed they were with the Ku Klux Klan. They took Schneider ashore, put a rope around his neck and let him swing a couple of times before letting him down. The men demanded that he tell them what he did with the stolen money. Schneider told them repeatedly that he didn't know where the money was, because he didn't steal it. They finally gave up and dragged him back to the boat. Captain Keith asked what happened. Schneider replied, "You know without asking." Schneider took his pay and left the boat at the next landing. On June 21, Missouri governor Thomas Crittenden offered a $150 reward for the arrest and conviction of the culprits who attacked Schneider.

On its trip upriver in mid-June 1884, the *Montana*'s captain was William Rodney Massie. Massie was a veteran riverboat man whose career extended from the 1840s into the early twentieth century.

Massie was born in Franklin County, Missouri, near the town of Hermann. His father knew the Boone family and claimed to have seen Lewis and Clark go by from their home on the riverbank. Massie's father had a woodyard that supplied fuel to steamboats operating on the Missouri. In 1842, Massie and his brother John were on a skiff when they saw the *Big Hatchie* blow up at the landing in Hermann. They helped to rescue survivors. Massie served in the Mexican-American War. He worked on several boats until becoming a pilot on the *El Paso*. In 1852, the *El Paso* was the first and only steamboat to ascend the Platte River as far as Guernsey, Wyoming. The next year, Massie piloted the *El Paso* up the Missouri River as far as the mouth of the Milk River (near present-day Fort Peck, Montana)—the first to make that trip also. His luck ran out in 1855, when the *El Paso* struck a snag at Franklin Island, White's Landing, near Boonville, Missouri.

After serving on various boats, Massie became the pilot of the *Spread Eagle*, a boat that earned a reputation for delivering cargo and passengers in record time. In 1862, the captain of the *Spread Eagle*, Robert Bailey, made a wager with Joseph LaBarge that his boat could beat LaBarge's *Emilie* on a trip from St. Louis to Fort Benton, Montana Territory. The race was close. Just as it appeared that the *Emilie* was going to win, Bailey ordered Massie to ram its bow. LaBarge threatened to shoot Bailey, and the

Spread Eagle backed away. Bailey lost his license over the stunt, and Massie was named captain of the *Spread Eagle*.

One of Massie's passions was poker. On August 2, 1876, between trips, he was playing poker at Nutaal & Mann's Saloon in Deadwood, Dakota Territory, with owner Carl Mann, Charlie Rich and another man. The fourth man left the game, and James Butler "Wild Bill" Hickok replaced him. Hickok asked Rich—who was sitting next to a wall of the saloon—to change places. Hickok was reputed never to sit anywhere except with his back to a wall. Rich refused. Hickok joined the men anyway. As the game progressed, Hickok was supposedly holding two aces and two eights when Jack McCall, with whom he had had an earlier dispute, approached him from behind. McCall drew a revolver and shot Hickok in the back of the head, killing him instantly. The bullet passed through Hickok's skull and hit Massie in the left wrist. Massie at first refused to testify against McCall, declaring that it might put his job in jeopardy and bemoaning the disgrace to his daughters for it to be publicly revealed that he was playing poker at a game where a man was murdered. He finally agreed to testify when a bench warrant was issued for his arrest. McCall was tried and hanged for the killing. Despite his initial reluctance to admit his participation in the poker game, in later years, every time his boat docked in Bismarck, Massie boasted that "the bullet that killed Wild Bill has come to town." Massie was buried in 1910 with the bullet still in his wrist.

Massie replaced the *Montana*'s usual captain, George Keith. The boat was bound from St. Louis to Kansas City with five hundred tons of freight, consisting of assorted merchandise, five hundred barrels of cement and six hundred barrels of salt. It was docked at St. Charles on June 22, 1884. The weather was hot. The river was high and rising higher and was running fast. A number of persons stood on the bank to watch the huge vessel push off from the shore and head between the piers of the Wabash Railroad bridge. A swift eddy caught the rudder, causing Massie to lose control. According to witnesses, the *Montana* struck the third pier from the St. Louis County (or south) side. Massie managed to beach the boat on the south shore in twelve feet of water. No one was killed or injured, but the boat was a total loss.

In the next week, salvors from the *T.F. Eckert*, hired by the insurance company, removed the freight and the fancy furniture and accouterments. About one hundred feet of the front of the boat's hull was removed and likely used to build or repair other boats. Its engines were removed and reused as well. Its bell was used at the Liggett & Myers Tobacco Company plant in St. Louis.

Steamboat Disasters of the Lower Missouri River

The *Montana* shortly after it hit the railroad bridge at St. Charles, Missouri, on June 22, 1884. *St. Louis Mercantile Library at the University of Missouri–St. Louis.*

The wreck of the *Montana* in June 1884 before the salvage boat *T.F. Eckert* arrived. *Murphy Library Special Collections, University of Wisconsin–La Crosse, La Crosse, Wisconsin.*

When the *Montana*'s sister ship, the *Dacotah*, captained by John Gonsallis, struck a snag at Providence Bend in September 1884, Massie asked, "Did Gonsallis not know an obstruction prominent as that stump in Providence Bend?" Gonsallis shot back that the stump was not as prominent as the St. Charles railroad bridge Massie struck. The *Dacotah*, unlike the *Montana*, was raised and continued service on the western rivers until 1893. Its hull was broken up into two barges, and its machinery went into the *Imperial*, which sailed on the Mississippi until it sank and burned in 1912. The *Dacotah* was best known for carrying the largest load of freight on the Red River in Louisiana when it brought 1,138 bales of cotton and 12,265 sacks of cotton seed to New Orleans in 1889.

The stripped-down hulk was left where the *Montana* sunk, and there it remains today. During periods of extreme low water, what is left of the hull rises like a ghost about two hundred yards upstream of the present-day Norfolk Southern and Interstate 370 bridges across from St. Charles. Only the port side is visible; the starboard side is buried in the silt and sand of the river.

The *Benton* (No. 2)

The *Benton (No. 2)* was built in 1875 for service on the Upper Missouri River. For twelve years, it plied the Bismarck–Fort Benton trade, making more trips and carrying more freight between those two points than any other boat. In 1889, it was sold to Captain James Boland—and its luck changed for the worse. On September 15, 1889, it was snagged in six feet of water five miles above Washington, Missouri, while carrying 5,000 sacks of wheat and 183 hogs. The hogs swam ashore, but the wheat was lost. Boland raised the boat and resumed the trade between St. Louis and points in Missouri. On July 31, 1895, while downbound near Arrow Rock, its tiller line parted, causing the boat to swerve into a snag. Sunk again, it lost 600 sacks of wheat. Undeterred, Captain Boland decided to take the *Benton* back to a happier place.

In 1897, the *Benton* began to run between Sioux City, Iowa, and South Dakota. On July 17, 1899, it returned to Sioux City with a cargo of livestock from Charles Mix County, South Dakota. It had, however, suffered some damage to its hull on the trip. Captain Boland received permission to take his vessel across the river to the government harbor on the Nebraska shore

Steamboat Disasters of the Lower Missouri River

The Sioux City, Iowa bridge tender failed to answer the *Benton (No.2)*'s whistle to open the bridge. This was the result. *State Historical Society of Missouri, Columbia, Missouri.*

because of work being done on the drawbridge on the Iowa side. As it pulled away on the evening of July 18, the *Benton* struck a submerged piling of the dike that protected the bridge from river debris, punching two holes in its side. Boland managed to patch the holes and believed he could get through the drawbridge to the other shore. Boland blew the ship's whistle to signal the bridge tender to open the bridge, but he wasn't there. By the time the tender returned and managed to partially open the bridge, the *Benton*'s stern had struck one of its piers, spun around and struck its side again. Boland managed to get through the bridge but had to beach the vessel on the Iowa shore.

Boland was incensed. His indignation was joined by other rivermen, as well as the influential *Waterways Journal*. The *Sioux City Journal* published an article about a U.S. Army Corps of Engineers report that condemned railroads for locating bridges "with little regard for any other interests but their own." Boland sued the bridge company and was awarded $4,500 in damages for its negligence in failing to open the bridge on time.

10
CAPTAINS AND CHRONICLERS

There were dozens of men who were riverboat captains on the Missouri River, but a few stand out. All came from humble origins and began their careers at equally humble jobs—cabin boy, deckhand, laborer at a woodyard, even shoe salesman. But they proved their worth and became famous among rivermen for their daring and skill. Even these captains, however, had to deal with disasters. Their boats were snagged and sunk, racked by disease, threatened with deadly fires, attacked by Indians and Civil War guerrillas, smacked into bridges, crushed by ice—in short, all the hazards that the treacherous river could offer.

The captains told many colorful tales (some were even true) that found their way into autobiographies and biographies. The fascination of river lore drew professional and amateur historians to study the development of steamboats, their technology, their economic effect on the settlement of the West and the people who ran them and rode them.

Grant Marsh

Grant Marsh was a well-known steamboat captain and pilot on the Missouri River for years. He became known nationally in 1876 for his role in taking the wounded from the Little Bighorn battlefield to Bismarck, North Dakota, in record time. Edward Godfrey, one of George Armstrong Custer's officers, described Marsh as "a man of tremendous energy and resources to fight and overcome all obstacles," traits that he exhibited throughout his life.

Marsh was born on May 11, 1834, in New York. His family moved to a small town on the Ohio River shortly thereafter. At age twelve, he was hired as a cabin boy on the *Dover*, an Allegheny River steamer. By 1852, he had worked his way up to deckhand on a steamer in the St. Louis–Louisville trade. He first worked on the Missouri River as a deckhand on the *F.X. Aubrey* running between St. Louis and St. Joseph in 1854. He began service on the *A.B. Chambers* as a watchman in 1856, when an ice gorge tore the vessel and fifty others from their berths, sinking several of them. Marsh was hired as a mate on the *Alonzo Child* and the *Hesperian* running to Omaha.

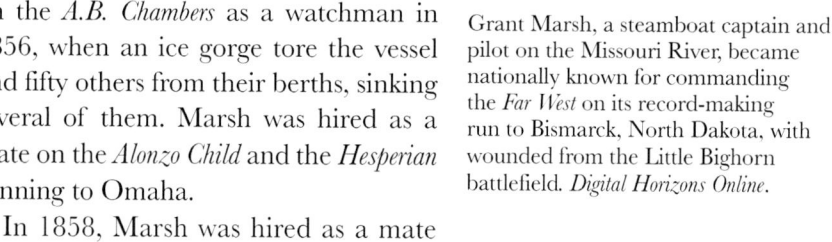

Grant Marsh, a steamboat captain and pilot on the Missouri River, became nationally known for commanding the *Far West* on its record-making run to Bismarck, North Dakota, with wounded from the Little Bighorn battlefield. *Digital Horizons Online*.

In 1858, Marsh was hired as a mate on the *A.B. Chambers No. 2*. He once again had a close call with menacing ice jams on the Mississippi, where the vessel was saved from destruction by one of its junior pilots, Samuel Clemens (Mark Twain). He and Clemens remained friends. Clemens left for Nevada Territory shortly after the Civil War began, but Marsh stayed in Missouri. He worked on a troop transport for Ulysses Grant's Tennessee campaign in 1862 and carried wounded from the Battle of Shiloh to Evansville and St. Louis.

Marsh made his first trip to the Upper Missouri as mate of the *Marcella*, one of a fleet of boats hired to take supplies to General Alfred Sully's expedition against the Sioux in 1864. His first command as captain was the *Luella*. In 1866, Marsh made four trips between St. Louis and Fort Benton. The Montana gold rush was in full force. Enterprising steamboat owners, captains and pilots could make huge profits hauling supplies upriver and gold dust downriver. For a time, Fort Benton was the busiest port between St. Louis and San Francisco. On September 2, 1866, the *Luella* left Fort Benton with 230 miners and two and a half tons of gold dust valued at $1,250,000 (in 1866 terms). It was reputed to be the most valuable cargo ever carried on the Missouri. Marsh brought the miners and their gold safely to St. Louis on October 5. The *Luella* cleared $24,000 on that voyage alone.

In 1869, the owners of the *Tempest* hired Marsh to quell a mutiny on the boat. The *Tempest* was grounded by low water. Trouble had been brewing after the engineer got drunk and killed an equally drunk passenger. When Marsh arrived at the boat, he found most of the crew drunk and the barkeeper issuing dire threats over their unpaid bar bills. Marsh decreed that no more liquor would be served. He regained control of the crew and soon had the boat afloat again. For his services, the owners paid Marsh $400 per month.

In the late summer of 1871, Marsh took the *Nellie Peck* downriver toward Sioux City, then the railhead for shipping supplies to Montana. He met a sister boat, the *Silver Lake*, coming upriver. The owners directed that Marsh should take over the *Silver Lake* and deliver its cargo to traders in Montana. He had not gone far back upstream when he tied up the boat for the night. To his surprise, the *Far West* soon tied up near him. The *Far West* was carrying a contingent of army officers the boat's captain was anxious to impress. Ordinarily, captains and pilots would take such an opportunity to exchange information about current river conditions, but the *Far West*'s captain chose not to do so, because, according to Marsh's biographer, the captain (identified only as "Rodney," perhaps William Rodney Massie) was reluctant to admit that "any one could be better informed than himself in a given situation."

The next morning, the *Far West* got away first. Being so late in the year, the river was quite low. The *Far West* proceeded around the outside of a bend in the river—the usual part of the channel that had the deepest water. But in coming down the day before, Marsh found that the channel had shifted to the other side and the deepest water was on the inside of the bend. Rodney apparently instructed his leadsmen checking the depth of the river to call out "No bottom!" regardless of what they found with their sounding poles. Marsh knew the water there could be no more than thirty inches deep. Suddenly, the *Far West* shivered and stopped. Marsh instructed his men to call out "No bottom!" as well. As they ran upriver in the deep part of the channel across from the grounded *Far West*, Marsh and his crew roared with laughter as the *Silver Lake*'s leadsmen bellowed "No bottom! No bottom!" Rodney was not amused and cursed Marsh as they went by.

Marsh was captain of the *Far West* himself during its most famous trip. The vessel was hired to support the army's 1876 expedition against

Steamboat Disasters of the Lower Missouri River

The *Far West* is famed for bringing wounded from the Little Bighorn battlefield from the mouth of the Yellowstone River to Bismarck, North Dakota—701 miles—in only fifty-four hours. It struck a snag and sank near St. Charles, Missouri, in 1883. *David Francis Barry Photo, Denver Public Library, Denver, Colorado.*

the Sioux for $360 per day. The *Far West* was built for use on the Upper Missouri by the Coulson Line. It was 190 feet long, with a 33-foot beam. Fully loaded with four hundred tons of freight, it drew only 4.5 feet. Unloaded, it drew twenty inches. It was primarily a freight boat, but it had cabins for thirty passengers.

Marsh took military supplies to Fort Lincoln (near Bismarck), arriving there on May 27. General Custer's wife, Libby, asked Marsh to allow her to travel farther upriver with him to be near her husband on the upcoming campaign. Marsh refused, citing the limited passenger accommodations. The *Far West* traveled up the Yellowstone River to the mouth of the Rosebud. There, on June 21, Generals Alfred Terry (the expedition's commander), John Gibbon (commander of an infantry and cavalry column) and Custer had a final council of war. Terry and Gibbon would march west along the Yellowstone. Custer would head south along the Rosebud and then west to the Little Bighorn River. The plan was to trap the Sioux between the columns.

Steamboat Disasters of the Lower Missouri River

Marsh was directed to bring the *Far West* up the Yellowstone and the Bighorn Rivers to the mouth of the Little Bighorn with the proviso that he not pass any point where the water was less than three feet deep, to avoid getting stranded. On June 25, Marsh and his crew noticed large columns of smoke on the southern horizon. They assumed it came from Indian villages the army was seeking to attack. The boat reached what Marsh identified as the mouth of the Little Bighorn at noon on June 26, but Captain Stephen Baker, the military commander on board, insisted that Marsh was wrong and that the boat travel farther up the Bighorn. Baker finally conceded that they had gone too far (convinced by Marsh's ruse that the river depth was falling below three feet—it wasn't). On June 27, they returned to the Little Bighorn. Curley, one of Custer's Crow scouts, approached the boat distraught. With some difficulty, Marsh was able to learn that Custer and all the men with him had been killed.

After a trying journey, fifty-two wounded men from Major Marcus Reno's battalion were brought on board. Marsh ordered fresh prairie grass to be cut, laid on the main deck between the boilers and the stern and covered with tarpaulins. The boat took on another passenger: Comanche, a horse belonging to Captain Myles Keogh and the only army survivor of the fight on what became known as Custer Hill. When General Terry arrived, Marsh rushed down the Bighorn, reaching its mouth in fifty-three hours. They waited two days for Gibbon's men to return. Fourteen of the lightly wounded were able to return to duty. On July 3, Terry instructed Marsh to take the remaining wounded men to Bismarck as fast as he could.

The *Far West* pushed off at 5:00 p.m. Fortunately, the river was high. Without stopping to tie up at night, Marsh ran down the Yellowstone and Missouri at full steam. The *Far West* scraped over the occasional sandbar and negotiated the many bends in the river. At 11:00 p.m. on July 5, Bismarck hove into sight. Marsh safely delivered the wounded and the terrible news of the Custer battle after traversing 710 miles in only fifty-four hours—a speed of 13 miles per hour. It was without doubt his most memorable trip.

Marsh continued to work on the Missouri for a few more years. He brought Sitting Bull to the Sioux reservation after his surrender. Then he returned to St. Louis and worked various boats on the Mississippi for twenty years. He returned briefly to the Upper Missouri, running the *Expansion* for the Benton Company. While employed there, he wrote letters criticizing officers of the company that were published in the *Waterways Journal*, a St. Louis–based magazine that was (and still is) one of the most widely read trade journals in the industry.

On August 23, 1907, the seventy-three-year-old Marsh boarded the *Expansion*, commanded by the seventy-eight-year-old William Rodney Massie. There had been bad blood between the two of them for years. Massie ordered Marsh to leave. He refused, and an altercation ensued. Massie later said, "I attacked him with a dangerous weapon, but it was only a sugar bowl. Of course, it was a pretty heavy bowl." Marsh was hauled before the licensing authorities. He claimed that Massie started the fight. The board, however, found him guilty of unprofessional conduct and suspended his license for a year. Marsh's friends sprang to his defense. Joseph Mills Hanson wrote a fiery letter to the editors of the *Waterways Journal* condemning the license authorities as ignorant, deceived or tyrannous. Hanson had more than the interest of a friend; he was in the process of writing a laudatory biography of Grant Marsh as one of the greatest river captains and pilots on the Missouri. The *Waterways Journal* editorialized that there must have been some undue "hypnotic influence" on the board considering the matter exercised by Marsh's former employer in retaliation for his public criticism of their officers. After all, it pointed out, Marsh was only defending the honor of his mother because he was "referred to (behind his back)…as a d——— s———."

Grant Marsh retired in 1910 and died at Bismarck on January 6, 1916. The I-94 bridge over the Missouri at Bismarck is named after Marsh. Riverside Park in Yankton, South Dakota, has a life-sized statue of him inscribed "Captain Grant Prince Marsh, 1834–1916, steamboat captain, pilot, riverman. 'He never flinched at the call of duty.'"

Henry Dodd

If some boats were unlucky, some captains and pilots were unlucky, too. Henry Dodd falls into this category. He was on board, piloting or commanding at least five steamboats when they met their end on the Missouri River. Dodd first shipped out with his father, James Dodd, in 1858. James was the owner of Dodd's Island at the mouth of the Osage River. The Osage Chute between Dodd's Island and the Missouri River shore was one of the most notoriously dangerous stretches of the river until the government filled in the upper end with revetments and dikes, making Dodd's Island a peninsula and extending the mouth of the Osage about five miles downriver.

Dodd was on the *Kate Howard* when it sank on top of the *Excel*, which had gone down two years earlier. The *Kate Howard* was hugely popular among the shore-based population, because it had a calliope on board. It was downbound from St. Joseph for St. Louis with a load of tobacco and hemp on August 4, 1859, when it hit a snag in the Osage Chute and sank opposite Dodd's boyhood home.

After service as a watchman on the *Deer Lodge* under Joseph LaBarge in 1867, Dodd was cub pilot on the *Post Boy* from 1868 to 1871. Dodd's favorite boat was the *General Meade*. The stern-wheeler was built in Pittsburgh for the Upper Missouri trade. It ran there until it was sunk by an ice gorge in 1881. It was repaired and returned to service on the Lower Missouri. It ran for several years carrying grain. Dodd was aboard when, on September 4, 1888, while carrying four thousand sacks of grain, it hit a snag and sank opposite Jefferson City. He was in command of the *Nadine* on the Osage River when it was struck by the *Emma*, a boat commanded by the former governor of Missouri, Joseph McClurg. The *Ella Kimbrough* was another unlucky boat Dodd was unlucky enough to be on when it struck tree stumps that collected together in the St. Charles Chute after being dumped back into the river by snag boats. This accident prompted the *St. Louis Republican* to complain that the government ought to find some other way to dispose of the stumps, because "otherwise the results of their labors will render the Missouri even more difficult and hazardous of navigation than it was before they commenced operations here." The U.S. Army Corps of Engineers listened but decided not to discontinue the practice.

Dodd prevented a disaster while a pilot on the *A.L. Mason*, one of three large boats built in 1890 to compete with the railroads in the St. Louis–Kansas City trade. The *A.L. Mason* was 252 feet long with a 56-foot beam and a hull only 6 feet deep. The river was running very high when the vessel approached the Wabash Railroad bridge at St. Charles. Two boats—the *Montana* and the *St. Luke*—had already met their ends striking this very bridge.

The *Mason* was so large that it had to lower its chimneys to pass under the bridge in high water. Dodd noticed, however, that neither the captain nor the mate had prepared to lower them. The captain was distracted by talking to some of the passengers on board. Dodd saw a large eddy swirling just above the bridge. He let the head of the boat enter the eddy, and then he started to turn it around so that it would pass under the bridge stern first. The captain called, "Hal, what are you doing? We don't want to land here."

Dodd replied, "I'm not going to land. I'm going to back this boat down through the bridge. I don't want the stacks to fall on the pilothouse."

Grant Marsh wasn't the only well-known riverman who commanded the *Far West*. Dodd became part owner of the vessel in 1883, along with Victor Bonnot, whose father built a mill across from Dodd's Island. The partnership in the *Far West* did not last long. It came down on its last trip in October 1883 heavily loaded with wheat, livestock, tobacco, barrel hoops and other freight. It landed at St. Charles to wait for daylight. The stretch of the river from there to the mouth was "always a dangerous piece of water." Dodd decided to hit the St. Charles bars; his brother Sterling (acting as pilot on this trip) stayed on board. About 2:00 a.m., Henry came on board roaring drunk. He woke up the entire crew and announced that "we are going down the river" for St. Louis immediately. Sterling pleaded with his brother to wait until daylight, but "whiskey made the old man brave."

Sterling went to the pilothouse and backed the boat into the river. About seven miles below St. Charles, near the head of Mullanphy Island, the *Far West* struck a snag in six feet of water and sank. The *Fannie Lewis* was nearby and took most of the cargo on board.

In 1940, Dr. E.B. Trail received a request from E.S. Luce, who was working on establishing a museum on the Custer Battlefield, asking if Trail knew of any part of the *Far West* that still existed to place in the museum. Dr. Trail replied that he was told by "Captain Farris of Jefferson City…that in 1917 he was in command of the snag boat *Missouri* that finally broke up the *Far West*, but that all the boilers and spare parts had been removed from the wreck before he blew her up."

Despite efforts by modern-day marine archaeologists, no one has been able to locate the remains of the *Far West*, probably the most famous steamboat that ever cruised the Missouri River.

Joseph LaBarge

Joseph LaBarge was born into a French Canadian family in St. Louis on October 1, 1815. Two brothers, Charles and John, also became steamboat pilots and captains. Both died in the line of duty. Charles was killed in the explosion of the *Saluda* on April 9, 1852. John died in 1885 at the helm of the *Benton* while it was leaving the landing at Bismarck. The captain noticed

Joseph LaBarge started as a clerk on the *Yellowstone* in 1832 and became one of the most famous steamboat captains on the Missouri River. He retired in 1885 but, with his vast knowledge, helped compile the definitive list of steamboat wrecks on the Missouri. *Missouri Historical Society.*

that the boat was drifting toward the bank. When he went to the pilothouse, he discovered John dead on the floor from an apparent heart attack.

Joseph was the second clerk on the *Yellowstone* on a trip to Louisiana, where he also served as a translator. He was on the *Yellowstone* later when it made its second trip up the Missouri, not as a crew member but as an employee of the American Fur Company. In 1833, he was left in charge of the *Yellowstone* at the mouth of the Kansas River after it was struck by a cholera epidemic when the captain traveled to St. Louis to hire another crew to bring it back. He began what his biographer Hiram Chittenden called his apprenticeship on a series of vessels that met unfortunate ends. The *St. Charles* burned at Richmond Landing (across from Lexington) in 1836; the *Boonville* was snagged in 1837 at the mouth of the Kansas River; the *Pratte* cruised without serious incident on the Missouri for two years but met its end thirty miles below St. Louis when it was snagged. He was the pilot on the *Emily* (1840), the *Omega* (1843) and the *Nimrod* (1844) and was captain and owner of the *Martha* (1848), which he contracted to operate for the American Fur Company.

LaBarge had some difficulty with the company and sold it the *Martha* after his last trip in 1848. He used the proceeds to build a new boat, the *St. Ange*. LaBarge contracted to haul government supplies to Fort Leavenworth, Kansas. On his second trip downbound in May 1849, the *St. Ange* was delayed by a severe thunderstorm. Instead of arriving at St. Louis in time to tie up before dark, it would not make the levee there until after midnight. When the *St. Ange* reached the mouth of the Missouri, LaBarge could see a glow in the night sky in the direction of St. Louis. When he reached the city, it was engulfed in flames—the Great St. Louis Fire. Finding nowhere to land, he went upriver a short distance and tied up on the east side. Over the next half a dozen years, LaBarge bought and sold several boats and continued to make voyages for the American Fur Company. That relationship ended for good in 1856. LaBarge spent the next two years running on the Lower Missouri between St. Louis and Council Bluffs.

In 1859, LaBarge built an "exceedingly beautiful craft," which he named the *Emilie*, after one of his daughters. The *Emilie* was a side-wheeler, 225 feet long, with a 32-foot beam and a hull 6 feet deep. LaBarge had many interesting experiences with it. Shortly after the *Emilie* was completed, LaBarge agreed with the Hannibal and St. Joseph Railroad to carry passengers and freight from St. Joseph to Omaha and Kansas City, as well as various points in between. In August 1859, Abraham Lincoln arrived at St. Joseph by railroad and took a steamboat to Council Bluffs to look at some land mortgaged to him as security for a debt. He was persuaded to make a speech on the slavery question. It was not received well by the local Democratic newspaper. He returned to St. Joseph the next day by boat. Lincoln returned in December 1859, once again traveling by rail to St. Joseph. He crossed to Ellwood, Kansas, and traveled through eastern Kansas to Leavenworth, giving speeches along the way. After a few days, he returned to St. Joseph by boat to catch the train home. LaBarge claimed to have met Lincoln on one of these trips, although he could not remember which one. Given LaBarge's contract with the railroad, it is likely that Lincoln traveled on the *Emilie* on at least one of his trips on the river, because that is what the boat was hired to do.

The *Emilie* was still working for the Hannibal and St. Joseph Railroad in 1861 when it first got caught up in the travails of the Civil War. LaBarge came down from Omaha and stopped at St. Joseph to pick up passengers and freight for points south. After the boat pulled into the stream, many of the passengers went to the upper deck and let out resounding cheers for Jefferson Davis. Someone telegraphed word of this to Leavenworth. The rabid Unionists there held a meeting and decided to hang LaBarge when the *Emilie* docked. Alexander Majors, one of the partners in the prominent shipping firm of Russell, Majors and Waddell, was in Leavenworth waiting to go home to Lexington. As soon as the *Emilie* touched the shore, Majors jumped on board and told LaBarge not to tie up or he would be hanged. LaBarge immediately backed the vessel off from the shore and proceeded downriver.

In June 1861, soldiers from the Missouri State Guard who had been routed by Union general Nathaniel Lyon at Boonville boarded the *Emilie* and demanded at gunpoint that LaBarge take their commander, General Sterling Price, who had fallen ill, to Lexington. LaBarge complied, but with misgivings, because he knew he had to face Union authorities when he reached St. Louis. Landing there, he was brought before General Lyon to explain why he had helped a Confederate general escape. LaBarge produced a letter from Price affirming that LaBarge had acted under duress. Lyon was not impressed. Lyon asked LaBarge if he knew anyone in St. Louis who could vouch for him. LaBarge suggested that Lyon speak to Frank Blair, an old friend, one of the prominent Unionists in the city and a staunch Lyon supporter. Blair convinced Lyon to release LaBarge.

LaBarge and the *Emilie* had one last adventure in the Civil War. Confederate colonel Joseph Porter came to Missouri in the summer of 1862 to recruit men for the Confederate army. After several skirmishes, he led about 300 men to Portland, Missouri, in southeast Callaway County. There, the *Emilie* stopped to drop off two passengers. The Confederate recruits were hiding in the wood pile. When the boat landed, they ambushed it and compelled LaBarge to unload its freight. Then, 175 recruits and horses boarded for the trip across the river. That was all that crossed, however. Federal cavalry caught up with the rest before the *Emilie* returned. The cavalry drove the Rebels away from the steamboat landing and chased them up the north bank of the river, killing 7.

The discovery of gold in the Montana Territory revived the Missouri River traffic despite the dangers posed by marauding guerrillas. LaBarge sold the *Emilie* in the winter of 1862–63 and bought the *Effie Deans*. The *Emilie* continued to ply the Missouri until 1868, when it was destroyed in a tornado that hit St. Joseph. LaBarge took the *Effie Deans* on several trips to the Upper Missouri transporting passengers and freight to the gold fields. In the winter of 1865–66, LaBarge put $6,000 in repairs into the boat. He advertised for a trip to Montana and obtained a full cargo. LaBarge debated whether to insure it for the trip. The *Effie Deans* was a stern-wheeler, which commanded higher premiums than a side-wheeler. He decided against it. The next day, April 7, 1866, it caught fire and was destroyed.

Undeterred, LaBarge next built the *Octavia* to engage in the Montana trade. It was a very successful trip, earning a $45,000 profit that paid off the cost of constructing the boat. LaBarge made another trip to Montana in the boat in 1868, then sold it to the U.S. government.

LaBarge spent $60,000 building his next boat, the *Emilie LaBarge*. Unfortunately, river traffic to the Montana Territory fell off. He made a trip to the Upper Missouri in 1870 and then confined the *Emilie LaBarge* to the trade between Omaha and St. Louis. LaBarge sold the boat for $30,000 in 1871. (It sank when it hit a snag in the Nashville Bend, below Providence, on June 4, 1874.)

LaBarge attempted to recoup his losses with a trip to the Red River in the *DeSmet*. It was a financial disaster. He made one last run to the Upper Missouri in 1877. Thereafter, LaBarge was the captain of the government steamer *Missouri*, which spent five years surveying the river. LaBarge left the river for good in 1885. He worked for the City of St. Louis for a few years. His last contribution to steamboating on the Missouri was to help Hiram Chittenden compile a list of the steamboat wrecks on the river. This list is still the starting point for any study of the subject (including this one). Joseph LaBarge died on April 3, 1899. He is buried in Calvary Cemetery in St. Louis.

JOSEPH KINNEY

Joseph Kinney got into steamboating much later than most of the prominent captains and owners. He was born in Washington County, Pennsylvania, on October 30, 1810. While a teenager, he worked in his uncle's packinghouse in Madison, Indiana. He invested in a steamboat in the New Orleans trade, but it was a financial failure. Kinney moved to Boonville in 1844 and opened a shoe store. This venture was much more successful and led to the opening of a second shoe store in St. Louis. He also got back into the maritime industry, building the *William H. Russell*, named for the Lexington merchant who became a successful freight hauler and part owner of the Pony Express. The *Russell* steamed the Missouri River for six years until it was destroyed by fire on the St. Louis wharf on October 27, 1862.

Joseph Kinney started as a shoe salesman and became one of the most successful steamboat owners. *State Historical Society of Missouri, Columbia, Missouri.*

STEAMBOAT DISASTERS OF THE LOWER MISSOURI RIVER

With the coming of the Civil War and later the Montana gold rush, Kinney invested in more steamboats. Kinney was friends with L.C. Ogden of St. Joseph. He offered to name his new boat after one of Ogden's daughters. Fannie drew the longest straw, and Kinney built the *Fannie Ogden* in 1862. The *Fannie Ogden* cruised the Missouri River until it burned at St. Louis on April 7, 1866. Kinney built two other boats during the war: the *Cora (No.1)* and the *Kate Kinney (No. 1)*, named after his daughters. The *Cora (No. 1)* was one of the first successful stern-wheelers on the Missouri River. It hit a snag and met its end in April 1865, a few days after and a few miles above where the *Bertrand* sank. It was replaced by the *Cora (No.2)*, built in 1865. The legacy of the *Cora (No. 2)* remains today in the form of Cora Island, created by sand and silt where the boat went down in 1869.

The *Kate Kinney (No. 1)* lasted a few years longer. It was partially burned in St. Louis in 1868 and burned for the final time in New Albany, Indiana, in 1872. Kinney built another *Kate Kinney* in 1873. It lasted until it also burned, at Shreveport, Louisiana, in 1883. The *Alice*, named after Kinney's youngest daughter, was sunk by a snag in September 1874. He built the *R.W. Dugan* in 1873 and operated it in the St. Louis–Kansas City trade until he sold it to Captain William Heckman Sr. Heckman ran it in the St. Louis–Rocheport wheat trade for a year and sold it back to Kinney in 1876. The *R.W. Dugan* hit a snag at DeWitt on October 31, 1878, and sank, with a total loss of its cargo of grain.

Kinney owned two boats that met their end in tragic collisions with bridges. The *St. Luke* hit the St. Charles railroad bridge on May 2, 1875. Kinney indulged himself in naming his boat built in 1872 the *Joe Kinney*. It was, however, an unlucky vessel with a disturbing affinity for bridges. A 231-foot side-wheeler with a 38-foot beam, the *Joe Kinney* struck the Missouri-Kansas-Texas Railroad bridge at Boonville, then swung under the south span, losing its pilothouse, Texas deck and chimneys. In 1876, it struck the railroad bridge at Kansas City, losing one of its paddle wheels. It was finally lost when, while upbound at Glasgow, it struck the railroad bridge there. Its tiller line parted, and the pilot lost control. It spun into a bridge pier and stove in its side. The vessel and cargo were a total loss.

With all these disasters to his steamboats, one might be excused in thinking that Joseph Kinney died a penniless and bitter old man. But one would be wrong. In between fires, snaggings and bridge collisions, Kinney's boats were financially lucrative. The *Cora (No. 2)*, for example, was one of Kinney's most successful boats, clearing a $50,000 profit on just one trip to Montana. When the Missouri Pacific Railroad bridge over

Despite losing many steamboats to snags, fires and bridge collisions, Joseph Kinney was so financially successful that he built this twelve-thousand-square-foot mansion, named Rivercene, in 1869, across the river from Boonville, Missouri. It is a bed-and-breakfast today. *Library of Congress.*

the Gasconade River burned, interrupting service from the east, Kinney started a ferry to carry passengers and freight from Hermann to Jefferson City, making $40,000 in three months. Indeed, he made enough money to build a mansion in 1869 across from Boonville, naming it "Rivercene." Rivercene is a twelve-thousand-square-foot brick manor, built in the style of the Second Empire Baroque Revival, featuring eleven imported marble fireplaces; walnut front doors weighing three hundred pounds each; a hand-carved mahogany, cypress, walnut and oak grand staircase; and eleven bedrooms. Rivercene remained in the family well into the twentieth century. It is now a bed-and-breakfast.

Joseph Kinney sold his last boat in 1882 and retired. He died in 1892, one of the most successful steamboat owners in Missouri.

Steamboat Disasters of the Lower Missouri River

River Historians, Amateur and Professional

How did a small-town dentist become one of the most celebrated historians—or, as he put it, "compiler"—of steamboats on the Missouri River? As with the captains and pilots whose stories he collected, E.B. Trail was fascinated with steamboats as a child. When a boat stopped nearby, he rowed from the family home at New Haven to talk to the captain and crew. He graduated from dental school at Washington University in St. Louis in 1905. In 1908, he took a hiatus from dentistry to work on the river with famed riverman William Massie. Trail's course was set. Although he returned to dentistry in Berger, Missouri, for more than fifty years, he logged 100,000 miles traveling up and down the Missouri River by boat and car to talk about the river with old-time rivermen, fellow historians and anyone with a poster, log, account book or any other document or photograph related to the Missouri River.

In today's world of the internet, digital and digitized photographs and documents, it is difficult to conceive of the time and persistence it took for Dr. Trail to assemble the immense collection that now resides at the State Historical Society of Missouri in Columbia. The Dr. E.B. Trail Collection there houses 279 folders of documents of all kinds, including more than one thousand original photographs. It has forty-one scrapbooks filled with clippings ranging from articles from the *Waterways Journal* to any item from the (now defunct) *St. Louis Globe-Democrat*'s feature "One Hundred Years Ago Today" that mentioned steamboats.

The Heckman family was another band of rivermen and women who not only worked on the steamboats but also wrote copiously about them, collecting river lore. William Heckman Jr.—who wrote under the name "Steamboat Bill"—was the son of a steamboat captain and a captain and boat builder himself. He was the author of *Steamboating Sixty-five Years on Missouri's Rivers: The Historical Story of Developing the Waterway Traffic on the Rivers of the Middlewest*. His niece, Dorothy Heckman Shrader, was also a prolific author. Their papers are also in the State Historical Society of Missouri.

Hiram Martin Chittenden was an army officer, historian and civil engineer. He was the author of two classic early histories of the West. *The American Fur Trade of the Far West* was published in 1902 and is described by Chittenden's biographer as the "standard overview [of the subject] and has never been imitated." Chittenden's *History of Early Steamboat Navigation on the Missouri River*, published in 1903, covered both the broader topic in its title and the life of Joseph LaBarge. He compiled a "Report on Steamboat Wrecks on Missouri River" in 1897 that detailed every sinking, fire, explosion

Dr. E.B. Trail, a dentist from Berger, Missouri, was a historian and "compiler" (his words) of steamboats on the Missouri River. He donated his collection of documents and more than one thousand photographs to the State Historical Society of Missouri. *State Historical Society of Missouri, Columbia, Missouri.*

and other calamity up to the time of its publication. He was assisted by LaBarge, Grant Marsh, William Massie and several other Missouri River captains. It remains an indispensable reference for any publication on steamboat wrecks (including this one.) Chittenden also plotted the location of each wreck on maps from the mouth of the Missouri to its headwaters. Dr. Trail supplemented the maps with his research. The results of Chittenden's and Trail's efforts were combined and are available today.

Louis Hunter was a professor of economics at American University. He spent twenty years researching memoirs, newspapers, state and federal statutes, business records, trade publications and technical journals to produce *Steamboats on the Western Rivers: An Economic and Technological History* in 1949. One commentator called it an "odd duck" of a book that another reviewer called "needlessly detailed." But that is only true if you do not want a single volume that covers every aspect of steamboat construction; commerce; and social, political and legal history. It is regarded as a classic that has not been equaled and remains the standard account of the industry.

William E. Lass is the author of several books on the history of the West, including two on the steamboat industry: *A History of Steamboating on the Upper Missouri River* (1962) and *Navigating the Missouri: Steamboating on Nature's Highway, 1819–1935* (2007). A professor emeritus at Mankato State University, he has written five books since retirement, the most recent being a history of his school completed in 2019 when he was ninety.

SEARCHING FOR TREASURE WHILE SAVING HISTORY

Given how many steamboats rest at the bottom of the Missouri River, many of which sank laden with cargo, it is no wonder that they are the stuff of dreams for treasure hunters. However, the hunt for sunken treasure in the Missouri River is plagued by many obstacles. The constantly changing channel often means that wrecks no longer even rest in the bed of the river. They are more likely to be buried under mud and sand in nearby farmers' fields. And just because the boat is now covered with dirt, water remains a problem, due to the water table, averaging six to eight feet below ground level. Today, there are also state and federal laws governing the ownership of any artifacts that are found, how the search and excavation must be conducted and how the artifacts can be dispersed.

In the early days, although gold and silver as well as the possibility of salvaging machinery were the stuff of treasure hunter's dreams, it was, as stated in the *St. Joseph Weekly Gazette*, something else that drove them to search the depths for treasure: "It has been told and retold that the manifests of these boats showed that the great bulk of freight in the holds consists of several hundred barrels of whiskey. It is for this fire water that people are now and have been prospecting and digging for many years. A bag of gold in the bottom of the river would not attract so much attention as all these barrels of whiskey."

The *Pontiac*

The *Pontiac* was headed upriver in April 1852 with a load of California-bound passengers when it snagged and sank with a reported cargo of several hundred barrels of whiskey. In 1882, a farmer named Walker claimed to have discovered the wreck buried in the sand a half mile from the channel. Yet, he recovered nothing. In the later years of the nineteenth century, several groups continued the search, with no results.

The *John Golong*

An old steamboat man named Caswell made the news far and wide—from Kansas to Missouri and from New York to Los Angeles—in the early 1880s with his tale of treasure on the sunken *John Golong*. He was a crew member of the steamboat *Ione* in the 1840s when they passed the *Golong* about six miles above Boonville the morning after its accident. The wrecked boat had, Caswell said, struck a snag and swung around broadside to the current. The snag held the boat tight as it careened on the larboard (today referred to as port or left) side and wrecked. According to the old sailor, the *Golong* carried $60,000 in gold in two iron safes bound for an upriver fort to be used to buy supplies and pay soldiers. The safes were so heavy they could not be raised or removed from the wreck. Caswell, despite earlier failed attempts, hoped to try to recover the treasure himself, but no results were reported.

The *Boreas*

There are successful attempts at recovering cargo from sunken steamboats, often after many tries. An unusual example of immediate recovery of treasure is found in the story of the *Boreas* and its destruction in March 1846.

The *Boreas*, with its cargo of wheat, tobacco, hemp, port and $80,000 in Mexican gold and silver belonging to a Santa Fe merchant who was a passenger on the boat, was traveling downriver and burned to the waterline below Hermann, Missouri. The story in the *Hermanner Wochenblatt* suggests that the fire was deliberately set in an attempt to steal the gold and silver. The watchman initially spotted a small fire under machinery at the front of the boat, and as he was fighting that fire, a second, larger fire broke out at the stern of the boat. This second fire immediately spread throughout the entire boat. Fortunately, all of those aboard escaped safely. Unfortunately, the gold was locked in the safe, and the clerk who held the key could not be found in the confusion of evacuating the steamer.

In the midst of the fire, a mass of melted silver was rescued from on top of the steam boiler. The crew cleared a path to the boiler, and some rescued the coin while others fought the fire. From the shore, according to the news reports, it appeared that those who saved the coins had run straight into the fire, and they were hailed as heroes.

At that point, the boiler sank into the river. The crew waited for it to explode as the hot metal met the cool water.

The owner of the money was not willing to part with the treasure and offered one-third of anything recovered to anyone brave enough to go after the coin. A few men came forward and, despite the danger, took the challenge. When they returned with gold and silver, the remaining crew jumped in. The newspaper likened the resulting scene to "buccaneers returning home richly laden from a voyage and resting from their labors."

THE *BERTRAND*

In the spring of 1865, William Wheatley and his brother-in-law Joseph Humes decided to seek their fortune in the gold fields of the Montana Territory. Wheatley, a cobbler, and Humes, a miller, were not going to mine, however. They intended to set up a sawmill to provide lumber for the sluices used to mine gold and to build the homes and businesses that were springing up. William and Joseph bought the machinery for the sawmill in St. Louis and needed a way to get it to Fort Benton, or wherever they could put it in operation. They contracted with a new boat that was sent to St. Louis, also to take advantage of the booming business of supplying the gold fields. The *Bertrand* had been built a few months before in Wheeling, West Virginia, for the Ohio River trade. But the Missouri River trade was much more lucrative.

As an Ohio River boat, the *Bertrand* lacked some of the characteristics of boats specially built for the Missouri River trade, such as the spoonbill bow sported by its sister vessel the *Deer Lodge*, but from the main deck up it was otherwise almost indistinguishable from Missouri River steamboats. The *Bertrand*, a stern-wheeler, had two boilers and engines salvaged from the wreck of the *A.J. Sweeney*, which hit a bridge and sank on the Cumberland River in March 1864. The *Bertrand* was originally named the *Argiota* when it was under construction but took the name it has been known by for more than 150 years at the time it was formally licensed to operate on the rivers. Its owners touted its carrying capacity and "most excellent cabin accommodations." The *Wheeling Daily Intelligencer* described the *Bertrand* as "a nice little steamer, neat but not gaudy and sits on the water like a duck."

The *Bertrand* was sold twice between its formal enrollment on November 25, 1864, and its last voyage. Ben Goodwin and Jeremiah Cochran sold it to James and John Yore for $40,000 on February 8, 1865. Sometime before leaving for Montana, the Yores sold a part interest to the Montana and Idaho Transportation Line owned by John J. Roe and his son-in-law John G. Copelin. It was common for a boat to have several owners, to spread the risk of loss. Roe and Copelin added the boat to their fleet, which included the *Fanny Ogden* and the *Deer Lodge*. In addition to having the largest and most active fleet of boats in the Montana trade, Roe and Copelin were prominent merchants in St. Louis and Montana. After quick trips to Cairo and as far up the Missouri as Leavenworth, the *Bertrand* prepared to make its first trip to Fort Benton, Montana Territory.

The *Bertrand* was blessed with a well-qualified crew. There were three experienced captains on board. James Yore, a part owner of the boat and of the Montana and Idaho Transportation Line, was a thirty-six-year-old Irishman who not only traveled the Missouri River frequently but also was a part owner of several boats in the trade in addition to the *Bertrand*. He was to command the boat from St. Louis to Omaha, from where he planned to return downriver. John Jacobs was only twenty-three, but he was also an experienced Missouri River pilot and one of the owners of the Montana and Idaho Transportation Line. By far the most experienced captain was Horace E. Bixby. He ran away from home at the age of eighteen to work as a mud clerk on the Ohio River. Two years later, he became a pilot on that river. He left to become the captain and pilot of the *Paul Jones*, where he took on a cub pilot named Samuel Clemens to teach him how to "read" the river. Clemens, writing as Mark Twain in *Life on the Mississippi*, described the thousand things a pilot had to know about the river and how many of those would change from day to day, if not from hour to hour or even minute to minute. Bixby, a strict taskmaster, sometimes would lose his temper and fill the air with oaths until "[y]ou could have drawn a seine through his system and not caught curses enough to disturb your mother with." But for the most part he was, or claimed he was, of "temperate habits" and "a cheerful state of mind." The boat's engineer was Albert Rowe Jr., described by historian Ronald Switzer as "one of the most highly regarded steamboat engineers of his time." He earned his reputation during the Civil War by installing engines on Union ironclads and converting steamers to gunboats.

Joseph Humes departed St. Louis on the *Deer Lodge* on March 16, no doubt to scout a location for the sawmill. Wheatley and a man named Wilson—possibly Humes's neighbor—followed on the *Bertrand* two days later. The number of other passengers on the boat is not known, but there were at least twenty and perhaps as many as forty on board.

Horace Bixby had the good fortune to be immortalized by Mark Twain in *Life on the Mississippi*. He had the bad fortune to be in command of the *Bertrand* when it sank. *Murphy Library Special Collections, University of Wisconsin–La Crosse, La Crosse, Wisconsin.*

Jerome Petsche and Ronald Switzer spent forty-five years studying the *Bertrand*, unearthing extensive information about its voyage, cargo, crew, passengers and consignees. Some highlights are discussed below.

Willard Barrows, a fifty-nine-year-old lawyer, surveyor, investor and author from Davenport, Iowa; his daughter, Caroline Millard; and Barrows's two young granddaughters were headed to Virginia City, Montana Territory, where his son-in-law, Joseph Millard, had established a gold exchange and a bank. John Atchison moved to Montana in 1864 and worked for Millard. He sent for his wife, Mary, and children, Charles and Emma, to join him in Helena. Captain Bixby's wife, Susanna, and their servant, possibly a Chinese woman named Yi-Shing, accompanied him. Annie Campbell celebrated her twenty-first birthday on the day of departure. Her younger sister Fannie, age eighteen, a woman described as having "charisma, charm, beauty," was also on board. The sisters had just finished boarding school and were headed to Montana to join their parents and younger brother and sister.

Foodstuffs were in short supply in Montana that spring, and Roe, Copelin and Yore loaded the steamer with a considerable amount of flour, sugar and potatoes, as well as pepper, mustard, horseradish and more exotic items, such as French olive oil, brandied peaches and cherries, and sardines. Besides Wheatley and Humes's sawmill, the *Bertrand* carried nails, saws, locks, various hand tools and plows. It also had military supplies, including gunpowder and artillery ammunition. The boat was reputed to be carrying five thousand gallons of whiskey in oaken barrels. Perhaps its single most valuable cargo were cast-iron containers that held as much as 35,000 pounds of mercury (worth more than $250,000 today) used to separate gold from impurities in which it is found.

The *Bertrand* made its way slowly up the Missouri River. It had to contend with numerous trees washed from the banks by floodwaters, their root balls having sunk to the bottom, leaving undetectable snags waiting to catch the unwary—or even the wary—steamboat. The *Bertrand* landed at Atchison, Kansas (about 470 miles upriver from St. Louis), at 2:00 p.m. on March 26, landed some passengers and freight and continued toward Omaha, another 350 miles via the twisting channel of the Missouri. The *Bertrand* tied up at Omaha on March 31. Captain Yore left the boat to spend the night at the Herndon House, the town's largest and most prestigious hotel. He left the *Bertrand* in Captain Bixby's capable hands and intended to return to St. Louis.

The stretch of river above Omaha was particularly treacherous. On March 28, the *Deer Lodge*, with Joseph Humes on board, tied up five miles above the Boyer River, not far from DeSoto Bend. The next day, it broke a flange on a paddle wheel from the debris encountered in the river. On March 30, it broke a paddle wheel on a snag just before nightfall. After repairing the paddle wheel on March 31, the *Deer Lodge* had a snag catch a hog chain on its boiler deck, which "carried it off and smashing things in general." On April 1, the boat struck yet another snag and broke the rudder again. The *Deer Lodge* also repeatedly ran aground in the same stretch of river when it wasn't being damaged by snags.

The *Bertrand* got underway at daybreak on April 1, working its way through the same snags and sandbars the *Deer Lodge* had encountered. By 3:00 p.m., it had made its way without any untoward incidents to DeSoto Bend, about twenty-five miles above Omaha as the crow flies and about twice that distance up the winding river channel. The day was warm and pleasant. The passengers lounged about, reading or talking to pass the time.

Without warning, a severe jolt struck the boat. A giant snag ripped through the hull just forward of the port paddle wheel. The *Bertrand* began to warp around the snag, driven by the current. Captain Bixby spun the wheel hard to port to beach the boat on the Nebraska shore. It struck a sandbar and

The *Bertrand* sinking after being snagged on April 1, 1865. After treasure hunters searched for it for decades, it was finally found in 1967 in the DeSoto National Wildlife Refuge. *U.S. Fish and Wildlife Service.*

listed so far to port that, as Willard Barrows later recalled, "chairs, tables and other furniture of the cabin were thrown to one side; glass ware, crockery, skylight windows and glass doors of the cabin were broken and creaking; the laboring vessel was parting and straining her timbers in rolling over." Eight-year-old John Edward Walton "climbed to the top deck right away....When it hit [the sandbar] it rolled part way over on its side and almost threw me overboard." Water rushed into the hull, and the boat sank in about seven to twelve feet of water in five minutes.

The *Bertrand* came to rest about thirty feet from the shore. Some passengers swam ashore. The crew immediately launched the yawl and made the boat fast to the shore with a line. They took passengers who gathered on the bow off in the yawl. Other members of the crew managed to rig a loading stage to the ladies' cabin on the stern, and the rest of the passengers safely left the boat. No one was hurt, but the *Bertrand* was a total loss.

The crew erected shelters from freight brought off the main deck and made the passengers as comfortable as possible by bringing carpets and furniture from the cabins. The cooking equipment was also salvaged, and the survivors were able to have hot meals. Some passengers made their way to the village of DeSoto, about four miles away, and may have stayed there for the night. Most of the passengers caught the next boat up—the *General Grant*—and continued their journey with whatever baggage they were able to recover. The crew returned to Omaha. Captain Yore postponed his trip to St. Louis to stay behind to assist in the salvage of the *Bertrand*. Most likely, he telegraphed his fellow owners and the insurance company to send men right away to recover as much of the cargo as possible.

Wheatley stayed behind to salvage the sawmill, but his traveling companion went on to Montana. Wheatley and Humes had not insured the sawmill, but he asked and received permission from John Copelin to have the men working for the insurance company retrieve it. Copelin offered to take Wheatley and his sawmill to Montana on another boat without further charge. Wheatley took him up on the offer and rode with his cargo on the *New Sam Gaty* to Fort Benton. But the condition of the river was such that he couldn't take the sawmill to Virginia City, Montana, in time to set it up before winter. Wheatley and Humes sold the sawmill and returned to Missouri in 1866. William bought Val-de-Moulin, his wife's family farm near Gravois Mills, Missouri, and Joseph resumed his occupation as a miller.

Willard Barrows stayed behind in Omaha as well. He caught a boat back to St. Louis, where he arranged for replacement goods to be shipped to Montana. He went home to Davenport for a few days and then left to rejoin his daughter, grandchildren and son-in-law in Montana. Caroline Millard was not happy in Montana and returned home to Omaha after a couple of weeks with her husband. She apparently convinced Joseph to return to Nebraska as well. He prospered as a prominent banker and was elected as a U.S. senator in 1901. Annie and Fannie Campbell remained in Montana and became prominent citizens there, Annie as a schoolteacher and Fannie as a rancher.

Yore and the insurance company salvors recovered the freight that remained on the main and boiler decks. They also likely dismantled the boat's superstructure to reuse the lumber. As was typical, the boilers, engines and other machinery were also salvaged to be reused. Although it isn't certain, Yore seems to have had the salvors cut a hole in the forward part of the boat to get to the mercury. If there were any barrels of whiskey on board, they were taken, too. The *Cora (No. 1)* hit a snag only two miles upriver from the wreck of the *Bertrand* on May 4, 1865, and went down in six feet of water. The salvors were pulled off the *Bertrand* and sent to the *Cora (No. 1)*, perhaps having recovered as much of value from the *Bertrand* as could be readily gotten.

The last contemporary report on the *Bertrand* comes from the diary of William Houston Gallaher of St. Charles, Missouri, who was taking the *St. John* to Montana. They came upon the wreck at 10:30 a.m. on April 9. It was "badly sunk to the cabin floor." Gallaher was surprised to see Annie and Fannie Campbell, who came to the wreck while he was there. They were waiting for passage on the *General Grant*. Gallaher's boat left after tarrying at the wreck for about an hour. At some point, the river covered the hull. The *Bertrand* would be seen no more for one hundred years.

Although unseen, the *Bertrand* was not forgotten. The lure of a possible treasure lying somewhere under the soil of the Nebraska bank of the Missouri River kept its memory alive. In 1896, at the suggestion of F.M. McNeely, who, as a seventeen-year-old, had helped to salvage the *Bertrand*, a group of Nebraskans searched for the lost boat. They consulted old charts, narrowing the area down to a three-hundred-by-one-hundred-foot zone. Their engineer then tried to find a spot to take borings by using a "dip needle" to locate metal mercury containers and other metal parts of the boat. The search, however, was unsuccessful. From time to time over the next seventy years, hopes of finding the *Bertrand* were revived by the changing of the Missouri River channel as it meandered back and forth when the spring and June floods brought high water down from the mountains and scoured long-deposited silt and mud off other steamboat wrecks in the area.

Bill Bennett, a New Yorker, alleged that he had a "divine gift" to find wealth in the Missouri River, especially that hiding under its waters near Blair, Nebraska, a town close to the area where the *Bertrand* went down. He offered to find the *Bertrand* for the city council. He said that somewhere under the sands was $100,000 in mercury and five thousand gallons of whiskey worth at least $27,000 waiting to be recovered. The *Lincoln Sunday Journal and Star* said that Bennett announced that "his is the art to bring treasure into 'God's sunlight,' and he is able, so he wrote, to 'read Mother Earth like a book.'" The council was not impressed and refused the offer.

In 1967, Jesse Pursell and Sam Corbino read of the earlier efforts to locate the *Bertrand*. Consulting the same old maps as McNeely's group, as well as land records and aerial photographs, they found a likely location for the boat. Pursell and Corbino used a flux gate magnetometer—a modern-day version of a dip needle that detects variations in the intensity of magnetic fields that differ from normal—to find the first physical evidence of a boat under the Nebraska soil. They took borings and located a steamboat wreck twenty-eight feet below the surface.

Steamboat Disasters of the Lower Missouri River

The Bertrand *was excavated in 1968–69. After thousands of well-preserved artifacts were collected, it was covered back up. The Steamboat* Bertrand *Museum at the DeSoto National Wildlife Refuge houses 250,000 artifacts recovered from the boat. U.S. Fish and Wildlife Service.*

Excavation of a steamboat wreck is no small feat. In 1968, Pursell and Corbino, with the cooperation and assistance of the U.S. government (required because the *Bertrand* lay within the DeSoto National Wildlife Refuge), first used a dragline to take off most of the soil above the boat. Because the wreck lay below the water table, it was necessary to install more than two hundred wells and pumps to remove enough water to allow the archaeologists to get to the hull and the artifacts it contained. And how many artifacts there were! In the few months the boat was uncovered, more than 250,000 artifacts of various kinds, ranging from bottles to children's toys, were found.

Researchers were able to trace many of the items to specific passengers. For example, salvors found a tin pony and cart and a set of building blocks that belonged to Charles and Emma Atchison. A chalkboard slate in a wooden frame with the name "Annie" carved on the top belonged to Annie Campbell. Archaeologists were able to link many of the thousands of pieces of merchandise to specific merchants, because the labels on the boxes in which they were found were preserved. And, yes, the salvors found mercury, but only nine cast-iron carboys with ninety pounds of mercury each. No doubt Captain Yore saw to it in 1865 that the rest had been recovered. And, no, there were no barrels of whiskey. Either Captain Yore and the insurance company removed them, or their existence was just a river story that made the rounds and got better with the telling.

The government decided to cover the *Bertrand* again once the artifacts were removed. For years, researchers have preserved the myriad goods taken from the boat. They are on display at the U.S. Fish and Wildlife Service's DeSoto National Wildlife Refuge in a specially built museum, which can be visited year-round (except when the Missouri River is flooded).

The *Arabia*

Several attempts were made to recover the steamboat *Arabia* before a final, successful salvage in the winter of 1988–89 by River Salvage Inc.

The *Arabia* was built in Brownsville, Pennsylvania, in 1853. It was 171 feet long, 54 feet wide and could carry up to 220 tons of cargo. The steamer came to the Missouri River in 1855.

On August 30, 1856, the *Arabia*, captained by William Terrill, left St. Louis with 130 passengers and two hundred tons of freight. Seven days later, the steamboat reached Kansas City, Missouri. On September 5, the *Arabia* left Westport, Missouri, in the late afternoon. As it approached Parkville, Missouri, the boat hit a snag that thrust ten feet into the hull. The boat tilted left, and water covered the main deck. Able D. Kirk, a newlywed on his way to Nebraska, recounted his version of the wreck as quoted in the book *Treasure in a Cornfield*:

> *One evening when many of the passengers were at supper the boat struck a snag. We felt the shock and at once the boat started sinking. There was a wild scene on board. The boat went down till the water came over the deck, and the boat keeled over on one side. The chairs and stools were tumbled about and many of the children nearly fell into the water. Several of the men on board seized the life boat and started for the shore, but they came back and the women and children were put in the boat. They called for a small man to go with the boat and I was small and I got aboard. The river bank at the point where we landed had been caving off and was very steep. I climbed out and pulled the women ashore. Horses and wagons came down from Parkville and took us to the hotel there that night. Many of the trunks and valises were taken off the boat and stacked up in the woods near the river. That night they were broken open by thieves, and all the valuables were taken out. We were taken on the steamboat,* James A. Lucus, *and when we went aboard, all that could be seen of our boat was the top of the pilot house. That sank out of sight in a short time.*

The officers of the boat when interviewed by the *Daily Missouri Democrat* reported:

> Arabia—*The officers of this boat, which was lost in the Missouri last Friday, arrived yesterday on the* Tatum. *From them we learn that the sinking was a very sudden affair. The snag struck her forward of the*

Steamboat Disasters of the Lower Missouri River

There are no known photos of the *Arabia*. This painting by Gary R. Luce hangs in the Arabia Steamboat Museum in Kansas City, Missouri. *Arabia Steamboat Museum.*

This painting of the *Arabia* sinking also hangs in the Arabia Steamboat Museum. *Arabia Steamboat Museum.*

boilers, pierced its way into the center of a lot of freight and lifted the deck several inches above its proper level. As soon as the boat was brought again under control, she was headed for the bank, but sank when she was about the distance of her own length from it. Two minutes only elapsed from the striking until she sunk. Of course the alarm and confusion which always attends the like sudden disasters, prevailed here, but the fears of the passengers were allayed by the presence of mind displayed by her officers. We are glad to know that the only life lost on this unfortunate occasion was that of a mule, which would have been saved but for its own obstinacy.

It is really a matter to be wondered at, how quickly boats which sink in the Missouri, disappear as a general thing. When the men left this boat, on Sunday morning, the water had reached her hurricane deck, on the starboard side, and it is supposed she will now be entirely out of sight. The river is not rising, but the boat is sinking in the sand.

Although there was no loss of life (except the mule), there were still losses for the *Arabia*. The owners of the *Arabia* lost a steamboat. They did receive insurance in the amount of $18,200. The merchants who sold the goods and the merchants waiting for those goods to stock their shelves lost income. Crew and officers lost wages. Passengers lost personal belongings to the river and to thieves, some of these belongings were the everyday basics needed for travel while others were the materials needed to start a new life in the West. The mule lost its life. The owner of that poor animal claimed to have tried to make it move off the boat, but it was too stubborn to leave. However, when the boat was uncovered by River Salvage Inc., the mule's skeleton was found with a tether still tied to equipment on the deck. The settlers in Logan, Nebraska, where a majority of the supplies were headed, had a difficult winter without those goods. Eventually, the residents of Logan deserted their settlement and moved across the river to Sioux City, Iowa.

The first known attempt to recover the treasures of the *Arabia* by unknown individuals in 1871 failed. The steamboat, at least a boat matching the date and location of the *Arabia*, was discovered, and the treasure sought was hundreds of barrels of whiskey reputed to be on board.

A second attempt was undertaken in 1877 by Robert Treadway and Henry Tobener. This team built a wooden coffer dam to fight the water, always the most difficult obstacle to overcome. After spending $2,000 and finding only one case of felt hats, they gave up.

Steamboat Disasters of the Lower Missouri River

Henry Tobener was part of an early expedition to find the *Arabia* in 1877. This is a family photo of Lizzie and Henry with their nine surviving children in the late 1880s. *Arabia Steamboat Museum.*

In 1880, an unnamed group of searchers used an engine to pump out the water surrounding the *Arabia*. Unfortunately for the treasure (read, whiskey) hunters, a storm hit and washed away the equipment, leading the group to abandon its pursuit.

Despite a rival hunter's claim that all cargo had been removed from the *Arabia* on its sinking, Gale Henson led yet another attempt to reach the steamboat in the late 1890s. Henson's team located the boat by using metal rods to probe where they suspected it was buried after a local farmer, who as a boy had seen the boat sink, pointed the way. After being made a partner, the farmer harnessed his horse, followed the plow lines to a turn row and pointed. He explained that the smokestacks of the *Arabia* had stayed visible until winter. Every time he plowed along the turning row that fall, he could see the stacks between the horse's ears, and he used the same method to relocate the boat for Henson.

After marking the boat's location, Henson and his team cleared the brush over the marked area and estimated that they would have to dig down twenty-four to thirty-six feet to reach the *Arabia*. The Henson expedition used a steel caisson pressurized with air to force out water. Workers would then descend and remove the sand. The team worked from December 1897 until March 1898, when they ran out of money and abandoned their search. (Note: the teams worked in winter, because the water was lower and the colder temperatures protected anything recovered.)

After reading a *Kansas City Times* story in 1921, F.D. Walsworth leased the land where the steamboat *Arabia* was buried in an effort to continue the search. Unable to find investors, Walsworth also abandoned the search.

In 1975, two veterans of the *Bertrand* excavation, Jesse Pursell and Sam Corbino, took up the search for the *Arabia*. The land where the steamer lay was then owned by Norman Sortor. His family had owned the land for 110 years. Many hunters had searched unsuccessfully, and more had asked to dig on his land before this. He agreed to this search if the land was restored to its original topography after digging and for 15 percent of the find. Sortor said he agreed to this search because he believed Pursell and Corbino were serious about their work and would meet his requirements.

The two men opened an excavation and spent several thousand dollars. When they could not positively identify the boat as the *Arabia*, they did not follow through.

In 1987, a company of avocational salvors (the preferred term to *treasure hunters*), was looking for a sunken steamboat to excavate. The initial Delta Research team consisted of Bob, David and Greg Hawley; Gene Smith; Gary Sisk; and Jerry Mackey. The Hawleys had spent time on the river their entire lives and were always looking for an adventure. The three worked in a heating and cooling business together. David heard about the possibility of treasure under the Missouri River during one of his service calls, and it was decided that this was the adventure they had been seeking. Their search eventually pointed to a vessel, the *Missouri Packet*, one of the earliest steamboats to sink in the Missouri River (circa 1820). They dug with heavy equipment through thirty-five feet of sand and used pumps to remove seeping water. The men recovered two boilers, the steam engine and barrels of spoiled pork before deciding to discontinue the excavation. In this first dig, the salvors used a backhoe and damaged the vessel, according to Smith and Sisk. They believed the team should have used shovels and excavated more slowly, causing less damage and preserving the historical value. The Hawleys and Mackey claimed that using the bigger equipment was a financial decision, to see if there was anything of worth to justify spending more time and money. The engine recovered from the *Missouri Packet* is on display at the Arabia Steamboat Museum in Kansas City, Missouri. The difference in opinion regarding the method of excavation caused a rift between Smith and Sisk and the Hawleys and Mackey, and they parted ways.

This steam engine was recovered from the *Missouri Packet*, which sank near Arrow Rock, Missouri, in May 1820. It is on display at the Arabia Steamboat Museum. *Author photo. Arabia Steamboat Museum.*

Despite the criticism and coming up empty in its *Missouri Packet* excavation, River Salvage Inc. continued with the Hawleys, Mackey and David Lutrell. The salvors considered and eliminated several steamboats before convincing Norman Sortor to allow them to dig for the *Arabia* under the same terms Sortor had set out previously.

In the summer of 1988, Sortor showed David Hawley where the other salvors had dug for the steamboat. Two hours later, David had located the *Arabia* using a magnetometer. After harvest, the team drilled, careful to touch only the boat and not damage the cargo. As they determined the outline of the boat using this method, they marked the location using flags.

The next step was to take core samples to determine whether and what cargo might still be beneath the earth. The first sample determined that the upper decks were no longer present and showed no sign of cargo. The second sample struck steel. The third sample found only a stack of pine lumber—cargo, but not the sort the salvors were searching for. Disappointment was growing. The fourth sample brought up fragments of red glass determined to be from a goblet and splintered wood bearing a lion crest from a chest of English Queensware. It was enough. River Salvage Inc. would excavate the *Arabia*.

Winter excavation would be hard for the team, but water levels would be lower, and the temperatures would help preserve artifacts. On November 13, 1988, the men broke ground for twelve electric submersible pumps necessary to rid the dig of water. On Thanksgiving Day, November 24, 1988, the River Salvage Inc. crew fired up the generators, and the wells began pumping water from around the boat—more water than expected.

The larboard paddle wheel appeared one board at a time on November 30. The dig continued after installing two additional de-watering wells, and the team unearthed the paddle wheels using a shovel on December 1. Mackey spotted a worn shoe resting on the boards of the wheel, and the men had their first artifact.

After excavating one engine, the doctor and three boilers during the first days of December, the top of a wooden barrel appeared on December 5, the barrel sitting on the main deck. Jerry Mackey pried the lid loose, and an assortment of dishes and glassware, nestled in mud, appeared.

Money was a constant worry as the search continued. The team originally thought $250,000 would fund the endeavor from start to finish. They spent nearly that much finding the *Arabia*. The men sought investors and borrowed money for more wells, equipment and fuel as well as storage and preservation space for the growing accumulation of artifacts.

And that preservation and storage of artifacts was another difficulty. Learning the process—quickly—was part of the problem. Another was that for all the years it was buried, the *Arabia* and its contents had existed in an oxygen-free environment with constant temperatures, no light and a neutral soil pH. To preserve them, the artifacts had to be stored under controlled humidity and temperature. Jerry Mackey's walk-in coolers and freezers (he owned restaurants) provided such an environment. A limestone cave was rented to store wood artifacts that had to be "watered" regularly as part of their preservation process. Leather and rubber items were frozen in blocks of ice until they could be properly dried and preserved. Fabrics—wool and silk—were misted with a light coat of water and frozen.

Greg Hawley said that recovering the artifacts was "like Christmas every day." The personal items for the move west were the most interesting—a child's toys and perfume, still fragrant. They found a small purse with two dimes and one half-dime (twenty-five cents)—practically all the money they found.

Guns were found buried deep in an inaccessible part of the cargo hold. Based on their research, the salvors wondered if they had been so hidden to smuggle into Kansas. On an earlier trip, abolitionists tried to do this, but the guns were found and confiscated in Lexington, Missouri.

The excavation of the steamboat *Arabia* uncovered many, many barrels and boxes of dishware, glassware and serving pieces. *Author photo. Arabia Steamboat Museum.*

The last artifact found, in early February 1989, as the equipment was being removed from the excavation site, was an 1856 copper cent piece, bringing the total cash recovered to twenty-six cents. On February 11, 1989, the water pumps went silent as the water seeped in to cover once again the remains of the *Arabia*. For the next three weeks, the team refilled the site with 200,000 cubic yards of sand.

The men of River Salvage Inc. were no longer treasure hunters. They decided the value of the artifacts was historical, not monetary, and that they should preserve and share them in a museum showcasing the largest collection—over two hundred tons—of pre–Civil War artifacts ever found. "The most priceless thing discovered aboard the *Arabia*," Greg Hawley stated in his book, *Treasure in a Cornfield*, "was not the cargo, but the story it told." Even Norman Sortor couldn't bear to break up that collection. He decided that, instead of 15 percent of the recovery, he would choose twenty-five artifacts, to give one each to his children and grandchildren.

The Arabia Steamboat Museum opened on November 13, 1991, at 400 Grand Boulevard in Kansas City, Missouri. Many of the artifacts are displayed, showing a bit of the story of westward expansion. There is also a conservation lab, where museumgoers may view the process of preserving artifacts.

Steamboat Disasters of the Lower Missouri River

This photograph shows only some of the keys recovered in the *Arabia* excavation. *Author photo. Arabia Steamboat Museum.*

The museum's lease expires in the near future, and a new location is being considered.

The excavation of the *Arabia* occurred before Missouri passed new laws governing shipwrecks and their recovery. Archaeologists criticized the methods used by River Salvage Inc. and the lack of standards in recording their findings on the steamboat. In his book about the adventure, Greg Hawley says it was difficult to find professionals willing to help them with their preservation efforts, due to the Hawleys' lack of credentials. Yet, they continued to search and received advice from European and Canadian conservators.

Greg Hawley died in a car accident in 2009, but his brother David and other members of River Salvage Inc. are seeking a new steamboat to explore. According to the museum's website, they are working on uncovering the *Malta*. The *Malta* sank in August 1841 at Malta Bend near the *John Golong*. It was full of Indian trading goods headed for the Upper Missouri and the American Fur Company. There are, as David Hawley says in a video about the *Malta* (available for viewing at www.1856.com), "many stories to be told."

STEAMBOAT DISASTERS OF THE LOWER MISSOURI RIVER

THE *TWILIGHT*

River Salvage Inc.'s former partners Smith and Sisk were also still in the treasure hunter/salvor business. After the *Missouri Packet* and their parting with River Salvage, they set their sights on the steamboat *Twilight*.

In the early morning of September 10, 1865, the *Twilight*, captained by William Massie, left the channel in a heavy fog, struck a sycamore snag and sank. Nearby farmers cared for the passengers until the next morning, when they were picked up by a boat and taken to Kansas City. The cargo the boat carried was reputed to be very lucrative—whiskey, wine, liquor and many general supplies. This cargo report made it a prime target for treasure hunters.

For several years, the *Twilight* rested on a log in the river and would be visible when water was low, adding to the speculation. In 1868, G.W. Mountjoy and G.W. Tevis spent twenty days and $3,000 searching unsuccessfully for the *Twilight*.

In 1874, local farmers built a coffer dam around the steamboat and used a steam engine to remove the water around it. The expedition ended tragically when the dam collapsed, killing one and injuring another.

In 1887, a "great rise" occurred in the river, creating a sandbar and burying the *Twilight* under many feet of sand about 180 yards inland.

Again in 1895, an attempt was made to claim the cargo of the steamboat *Twilight*. Three Kansas City men—Captain Arthur Leopold, a riverboat pilot; Captain George R. Collins, a soldier; and John King, a machinist—joined forces to form the Kansas City Wrecking Company. In addition to the whiskey story, a rumor emerged regarding "specie" aboard the steamer. In one story, the money belonged to a woman who was moving a generous inheritance from the East to Kansas City. An alternate story had gold headed for army pay and to western merchants. Regardless, the possibility of lost gold added to the temptation to pursue any treasure aboard the boat.

A local farmer who witnessed the sinking as a young boy helped the men locate the *Twilight* by using landscape points to mark the original locale where the boat sank. Once the boat was located, the company lowered a caisson, which removed mud, water and sand using compressed air until it reached the metal of the steamboat's machinery. The machinery was removed, the deck was cut open and there it was: "The men were wild with delight down in the hold of the buried boat, with thirty-nine feet of wet sand above them. They filled their lungs with air pumped from above and rolled and danced and shook hands with one another."

And they found liquor—first thing! The liquor was white with a "piney odor." The bottle labels were gone, but the case was marked "Old London Club Gin 1860."

The men took the liquor to a Kansas City club for testing. When the white liquor was tasted, "a glow stole through the drinkers which spread from their toes to the tips of their ears, and they told voluminously of the good quality of this gin." And in examining the square-faced bottle holding the gin, one club man declared it was the same gin Charles Dickens wrote about and preferred. The estimate was floated that the liquor would sell for unheard-of amounts.

The company proceeded to unload the hold of its cargo, finding cans of spoiled food, bags of spoiled coffee, allspice that was still good, ten bags of peanut shells (the peanuts were gone) and twelve bales of jute.

By summer, the steam pump the company was using could no longer keep the water out of the boat. The men had not yet found their treasure-trove of whiskey, so they sank a second steel caisson over the front hatch. The crew uncovered more Old London Gin, Manhattan cocktail, clocks, mackerel (spoiled), machine supplies, rubber belting, knives, dog collars, guns, flasks and gunsmith tools.

Finally, in December 1895, when a wall of sand caved in, the men found more cases of gin and barrels of whiskey. There was not as much as hoped for, but what was there exceeded "anything in the whisky [sic] line they had ever dreamed of," according to the Kansas City club tasters. When the bottle was opened, it was said to fill the room with its aroma. It was also described as "thick and oily," almost the consistency of molasses. And when the glass was empty, the remainder clung to the sides "as sirup [sic] would."

There was a concern among the men involved in salvaging the cargo that there might be a tax problem with the liquor, so they left it on board the boat. They hoped there would be proof that taxes had already been paid at the distillery, but until they knew…

John King, a principal in the Kansas City Wrecking Company, ultimately declared their *Twilight* expedition a failure. No whiskey was recovered for fear the barrels would prove unstable and for fear of how tax officials would react. No cargo was valuable enough to recoup the costs of the recovery process.

Attempts in the early twentieth century to recover the *Twilight*'s treasures (whiskey) came to naught, but toward the end of the century, former River Salvage Inc. partners Gene Smith and Gary Sisk decided they would attempt to excavate the boat. This excavation would be more difficult than previous attempts, due to tougher laws concerning shipwrecks and their recovery, passed in part because of the *Missouri Packet* debacle.

The *Twilight* was now located on land overseen by the U.S. Army Corps of Engineers, near a protected wetland. The team hired a botanist to prepare an impact statement. They also had to have a state-approved archaeologist on board, and that archaeologist was required to document artifacts and where they were found. It took eighteen months to obtain the necessary permits. The men formed *Twilight* Management Inc. with a third partner, Wayne Roberts, in 1997 and began looking for investors.

The steamboat *Twilight* passed by St. Charles, Missouri, on its first voyage up the Missouri River in 1865, and St. Charles had a steamboat past. The partners sought money from the city for the excavation, but the city refused, because it was a use of public money for an unknown result. The excavation proceeded despite the lack of help from a public entity.

The partnership originally hoped to raise the *Twilight* in its entirety. Because it would be very heavy, they planned to cut and raise it in sections. The men wanted to do everything under proper standards and insisted that this expedition was not a treasure hunt but rather a preservation of history.

Although the *Arabia*'s cargo had already been raised, preserved and displayed, also adding to historical knowledge, there were important differences in the cargoes. The *Arabia* presented pre–Civil War life; the *Twilight* sank after the Civil War. For example, the *Arabia* cargo had hundreds of pairs of shoes pegged and made to fit either foot. Shoes from the post–Civil War era were stitched and designed to fit right and left feet.

The *Twilight* excavation resulted in much of the boat and its machinery being removed from the site. Artifacts recovered included Old London Club Gin, tools, stoves, kitchen implements, food and jewelry. In May 2001, the remains and artifacts were transported on three flatbed trailers to St. Charles to a building on the American Car Foundry campus for cleaning and storage. *Twilight* Management Inc. was interested in creating a museum in a river town. St. Charles, the city that refused to fund the excavation, was one of their choices. The city was interested, but the museum project came to nothing.

Twilight Management Inc. eventually had legal problems, and Gary Sisk took possession of the artifacts and stored them near Kansas City, Missouri, still hoping to create a museum. When the authors traveled in June 2019 to the site given as the address of the Twilight Steamboat Museum, the building was empty and no further information could be located.

BIBLIOGRAPHY

Albany (MO) Ledger. "Boatload of Whisky Submerged for Thirty Years Just Recovered." March 13, 1896.
Alton (IL) Evening Telegraph. "Loss of Steamer Judith." July 30, 1888.
Annual Report of the Adjutant General of the State of Missouri, 1863. Reprinted in the appendix to *Journal of the Senate of Missouri, Twenty-Second General Assembly.* Jefferson City, MO: J.P. Ament, 1863.
Annual Report of the Secretary of the Treasury on the State of Finances, 1860.
Atchison (KS) Daily Champion, March 26, 1865; May 20, 1865.
Barrows, Willard, "Three Thousand Miles Up the Missouri River by Willard Barrows." *Boston Review* 5, no. 29 (December 1865).
Binkley, Peter. *Wheatley Family History Project.* Accessed June 12, 2019. https://www.wallandbinkley.com/wheatley.
Bismarck (ND) Tribune. "Captain Grant Marsh." June 20, 1908.
———. "A Full Report of the Haps and Mishaps Which Go to Make Up the Life of Up-River Men." May 12, 1882.
———. "Sick, Died, Murdered and Lynched." May 26, 1882.
Black, W.H. "Letter to the Editor." *Leavenworth (KS) Times,* September 1, 1865.
Blackmar, Frank Wilson. *Kansas: A Cyclopedia of State History.* Chicago: Standard Publishing, 1912.
Bozeman (MT) Avant Courier. "McCall's Trial." December 22, 1876.
Chappell, Phil E. *A History of the Missouri River.* Kansas City, MO: Bryant & Douglas Book & Stationery Company, 1905. Kindle edition.

Bibliography

Chicago (IL) Tribune, February 23, 1866; June 15, 1866; July 11, 1866.

———. "Negro Roustabouts Badly Frozen." December 4, 1886.

Chittenden, Hiram Martin. *A History of Early Steamboat Navigation on the Missouri River: Life and Adventures of Joseph LaBarge*. New York: Francis P. Harper, 1903.

———. "Report on Steamboat Wrecks on the Missouri River." *Annual Report of the Missouri River Commission*. Washington, D.C.: Government Printing Office, 1897.

Cincinnati Enquirer. February 8, 1865.

Clavin, Tom. *Wild Bill: The True Story of the American Frontier's First Gunfighter*. New York: St. Martin's Press, 2019.

Corbin, Annalies, and Bradley R. Rogers. *The Steamboat Montana and the Opening of the West: History, Excavation, and Architecture*. Gainesville: University Press of Florida, 2008.

Daily Missouri Democrat (St. Louis). September 11, 1856.

Daily Missouri Republican (St. Louis). March 18, 1863; March 21, 1863; March 22, 1863; March 23, 1863.

Dickens, Charles. *American Notes and Pictures from Italy*. London: Chapman & Hall, 1898.

East Carolina University Maritime History Program: St. Charles Steamboat Project. www.archive.org.

Edwards, John Newman. *Noted Guerrillas, or the Warfare on the Border*. St. Louis, MO: Bryan, Brand & Company, 1877.

Evening News (Emporia KS), December 8, 1879.

Fisher, H.D. *The Gun and the Gospel: Early Kansas and Chaplain Fisher*. 2nd ed. Chicago and New York: Medical Century Company, 1897.

Fort Scott (KS) Daily Monitor. "Revenge." July 17, 1881.

Freeman, Darren. "Recovered Riverboat Reveals a Bit of History." *St. Louis Post-Dispatch*, April 30, 2001.

Gallipolis (OH) Journal. "Storm on the Missouri and Illinois Rivers—Steamer New Lucy Damaged." October 12, 1854.

Ganey, Terry. "Twilight Zone: Sunken Steamboat May Surface." *St. Louis Post-Dispatch*, September 8, 1995.

Giffen, Lawrence, Everett. *"Walks on Water": The Impact of Steamboating on the Lower Missouri River*. Jefferson City, MO: Giffen Enterprises, 2001.

Gillespie, Michael. *Wild River Wooden Boats*. Stoddard, WI: Heritage Press, 2000.

Glasgow (MO) Weekly Times. October 1, 1857.

———. "Another Steamboat Disaster." April 29, 1852.

BIBLIOGRAPHY

———. "Snagged." March 19, 1857.
———. "Steamboat Accident." August 5, 1852.
———. "Steamboating—*New Lucy*—Fast Time." July 13, 1854.
———. "Steamer *New Lucy* Burned." December 3, 1857.
———. "Steamer *Timour* Blown Up." August 31, 1854.
———. "Steamer *Timour* Sunk." December 8, 1853.
———. "Terrible Steamboat Accident." November 19, 1857.
Gordon, Christopher Alan. *Fire, Pestilence and Death: St. Louis 1849*. St. Louis: Missouri Historical Society Press, 2018.
Green, Clark H. "Letter to the Editor." *Glasgow (MO) Weekly Times*, October 5, 1854.
Gregg, William H. "A Little Dab of History Without Embellishment." State Historical Society of Missouri, Columbia, Missouri.
Gregory, Ralph. *History of Washington MO*. Washington, MO: Washington Preservation Inc. and Washington Historical Society, 2000.
Griffith, Cecil R., comp. *The Missouri River: The River Rat's Guide to Missouri River History and Folklore*. Leawood, KS: Canfield and Sanders, 1974.
Hall, John R. "One of Missouri's Little Known Battles Recalled by Glasgow's Bill against the U.S." *Kansas City (MO) Times*, July 25, 1952.
Hamilton, Jean Tyree. *Abel J. Vanmeter, His Park and His Diary*. Marshall, MO: Friends of Arrow Rock, 1972.
Hannibal (MO) Journal. February 24, 1853.
———. "Destructive Fire—Three Boats Burned." January 27, 1853.
Hanson, Joseph Mills. *The Conquest of the Missouri: Being the Story of the Life and Exploits of Captain Grant Marsh*. Chicago: A.C. McClurg, 1909.
Hartley, William G., and Fred E. Woods. *Explosion of the Steamboat Saluda: A Story of Disaster and Compassion Involving Mormon Emigrants and the Town of Lexington, Missouri, in April 1852*. Salt Lake City, UT: Millennial Press, 2002.
———. "Explosion of the Steamboat *Saluda*: Tragedy and Compassion at Lexington, Missouri, 1852." *Missouri Historical Review* 99 (July 2005): 281.
Hawley, Greg. *Treasure in a Cornfield*. Kansas City, MO: Paddlewheel Publishing, 2005.
Heckman, William L. ("Steamboat Bill"). *Steamboating Sixty-five Years on Missouri's Rivers: The Historical Story of Developing the Waterway Traffic on the Rivers of the Middlewest*. Kansas City, MO: Burton Publishing Company, 1950.
Henry, William. *Pension File*. National Archives and Records Administration. Copy in author's collection.

BIBLIOGRAPHY

Hereford, Robert A. "Old Man River—Gold Rush by Steamboat." *St. Louis Post-Dispatch*, June 11, 1943.

———. "Old Man River—Race Up the Missouri." *St. Louis Post-Dispatch*, June 14, 1943.

Hermanner Wochenblatt (Hermann, MO). March 8, 1846.

History of Lafayette County. St. Louis: Missouri Historical Company, 1881.

Hunter, Louis C. *Steamboats on the Western Rivers: An Economic and Technological History*. New York: Dover Publications, 1993.

Jackson, Donald. *Voyages of the Steamboat Yellow Stone*. Norman: University of Oklahoma Press, 1985.

Jacksonville (IL) Republican. August 10, 1842.

Johnson, Thomas B. *Union Provost Marshal's File of Papers Relating to Individual Civilians*. National Archives and Records Administration, RG 109, M345, Roll 101. www.Fold3.com.

Kane, Adam I. *The Western River Steamboat*. College Station: Texas A&M Press, 2004.

Kansas City (MO) Star. May 8, 2001.

Kansas City (MO) Times. "In Kansas City Forty Years Ago." April 16, 1920.

———. "Omaha Men Find More Proof of Sunken Steamboat." April 19, 1974.

Kansas Semi-Weekly Capital (Topeka). "Digging for Whisky." March 8, 1898.

Kearney (NE) Daily Hub. July 24, 1897.

Kinney, Cora. Letter to E.B. Trail, dated January 29, 1940. State Historical Society of Missouri E.B. Trail Collection.

KPLR Television. "The Steamboat Montana Resurfaces in the Missouri River." August 10, 2012. http://kplr11.com.

Lamoille (VT) Standard. "Dreadful Steamboat Explosion on Western Waters." July 23, 1842.

Lass, William E. *Navigating the Missouri: Steamboating on Nature's Highway, 1819–1935*. Norman, OK: Arthur H. Clark, 2008.

Launer, Louis J. "Boat Strikes Bridge—History Repeats Itself." *St. Charles Heritage* 8, no. 3 (July 1990): 15–18, 24.

Lawrence (KS) Tribune. "Guerrillas at Rocheport." September 15, 1864.

Leavenworth (KS) Daily Commercial. "Sinking of the Mollie Dozier." October 9, 1866.

Leavenworth (KS) Times. February 21, 1865; February 1, 1888.

———. "Robbed." August 31, 1865.

Lexington (MO) Intelligencer. November 29, 1879; June 21, 1884; July 12, 1884.

———. "A Strange Case," May 24, 1884.

Bibliography

Lincoln (NE) Journal Star. September 17, 1888.

Lincoln (NE) Sunday Journal and Star. February 7, 1937.

Lloyd, James T. *Lloyd's Steamboat Directory and Disasters on the Western Waters*. Cincinnati, OH: James T. Lloyd & Co., 1856.

Manning, Chandra. *Troubled Refuge: Struggling for Freedom in the Civil War*. New York: Alfred A. Knopf, 2016.

Massie, Captain William Rodney at http://www.steamboats.org/history-education/capt-william-rodney-massie.html.

McDonald, W. J. "The Missouri River and Its Victims: Vessels Wrecked from the Beginning of Navigation to 1925." Part I. *Missouri Historical Review* 21 (January 1927): 215.

———. "The Missouri River and Its Victims: Vessels Wrecked from the Beginning of Navigation to 1925." Part II. *Missouri Historical Review* 21 (April 1927): 455.

———. "The Missouri River and Its Victims: Vessels Wrecked from the Beginning of Navigation to 1925." Part III. *Missouri Historical Review* 21 (July 1927): 581.

Memphis (TN) Daily Appeal. March 7, 1863.

Milwaukee (WI) Sentinel. August 4, 1845.

Morgan, George H. *Annual Statement of the Trade and Commerce of Saint Louis for the Year 1868*. St. Louis, MO: H.P. Studley and Company, 1869.

Morning Democrat (IA). March 8, 1865; April 4, 1865.

New York Daily Herald. "Burning of the Steamer New Lucy." December 1, 1857.

New York Times. "The Missouri River: A Correct Statement of Distances—Old Figures Set Aside." August 30, 1869.

Omaha Daily Bee. July 19, 1896.

Parsons (KS) Daily Eclipse. "Steamboat Mate Killed." July 28, 1888.

Parsons (KS) Weekly Sun, "Lost Treasure." May 17, 1883.

Paskoff, Paul F. *Troubled Waters: Steamboat Disasters, River Improvements, and American Public Policy, 1821–1860*. Baton Rouge: Louisiana State University Press, 2007.

PastPorts. "St. Louis Cholera Epidemic of 1849." St. Louis County Library, December 2017/January 2018.

Petsche, Jerome E. *The Steamboat Bertrand History, Excavation, and Architecture*. Washington, D.C., National Park Service, U.S. Department of the Interior, 1974.

Republican Banner (TN). "Explosion of Steamer Sam Gaty—One Man Killed—Eleven Persons Wounded." April 13, 1860.

Bibliography

Riley, Patrick, *Union Citizens File*, RG 109, M345, Roll 230, National Archives and Records Administration.

Robertson, Tommy. "Museum Is Key to Steamboat's Final Home." *St. Charles (MO) Journal*, May 2, 2001.

Schuttner, Eberhardt. *Pension File*, National Archives and Records Administration. Copy in author's collection.

Sedalia (MO) Democrat. "O.K." May 5, 1875.

Sinisi, Kyle S. *The Last Hurrah: Sterling Price's Missouri Expedition of 1864*. Lanham, MD: Rowman & Littlefield, 2015.

Sioux City (IA) Journal. July 26, 1897.

———. "The Benton Is Sunk." July 19, 1897.

———. "Charles Mix Live Stock." July 18, 1897.

———. "Effects on Navigation." January 1, 1898.

———. "$4,500 for Damages to His Boat." June 25, 1899.

———. "It Roasts the Bridges." July 28, 1897.

———. "Opened a Whisky Mine." December 14, 1895.

———. "Piloting on the Missouri." August 18, 1901.

Smoky Hill and Republican Union (Junction City, KS). March 28, 1863.

Southern Argus (Selma, AL). July 19, 1842.

Southern Shield (Helena, AR). July 30, 1842.

Squatter Sovereign (Atchison, KS). "Pleasure Party on the New Lucy." July 31, 1855.

Spirit of Democracy (OH). August 16, 1845.

St. Charles (MO) Banner. "Shifting Sand Uncovers Remains of Packet Boat Sunk Here in 1884." November 3, 1964.

St. Charles (MO) Cosmos. July 2, 1884.

———. "The Montana Sunk." June 25, 1884.

St. Joseph (MO) Morning Herald. April 1, 1863; April 3, 1863; April 9, 1863; April 25, 1863.

———. "Digging for Whisky." May 18, 1889.

———. "The Pontiac—Two Hundred Barrels of Whisky Forty Years Old." February 7, 1882.

———. "To Be Hanged." January 28, 1882.

St. Joseph (MO) Weekly Gazette. "The Sunken *Arabia*." December 14, 1897.

St. Joseph (MO) Weekly Herald. "A Steamboat Mate Cowardly Murdered." August 2, 1888.

———. "The St. Louis Ice Gorge Charges against the Steamboat Men." February 9, 1888.

St. Louis Globe Democrat. December 7, 1907.

———. "The Ice Gorge." January 27, 1888.

Bibliography

St. Louis Post-Dispatch. "Another Suit for Damages." October 30, 1877.
———. "The Boat Strikes the St. Charles Bridge—Loss and Insurance." June 23, 1884
———. "Heavy Damages." October 31, 1877.
———. "Man Shot on the *Lady Lee*." August 8, 1881.
———. "The *Mollie Dozier* Parted." December 14, 1866.
———. "A Mysterious Murder." September 12, 1890.
———. "On Board the *Judith*." July 28, 1888.
———. "The Rivers." June 21, 1884.
———. "The Rivers." June 23, 1884.
———. "Seven Feet of Water." September 16, 1888.
———. "The Steamer Shooting." September 16, 1890.
———. "The Steamer *St. Luke* Wrecked on the Missouri." May 3, 1875.
———. "Struck a Sang and Sunk." September 16, 1889.
———. "Whose Case Is It?." September 14, 1890.
St. Louis Republic. "Raising the *Twilight*'s Cargo." December 1, 1895.
St. Louis Republican. January 20, 1853; November 23, 1857; January 13, 1866; August 6, 1881.
St. Louis Weekly Reveille. "Before Justice Cruess." August 25, 1845.
———. "The Big Hatchee." August 8, 1845.
———. "Dreadful Steamboat Explosion." July 28, 1845.
Switzer, Ronald R. *The Steamboat Bertrand and Missouri River Commerce*. Norman, OK: Arthur H. Clark, 2013.
Times-Picayune (New Orleans, LA). September 26, 1884.
———. "Another Fatal Steamboat Accident." August 1, 1845.
Trail, E.B. Handwritten scrip to *Waterways Journal*. November 11, 1937. State Historical Society of Missouri E.B. Trail Collection.
Twain, Mark (Samuel Clemens). *Life on the Mississippi*. New York: Harper & Brothers, 1901.
———. *Roughing It*. New York: Harper & Brothers, 1913.
Unruh, John Jr. *The Plains Across: The Overland Immigrants and the Trans-Mississippi West, 1840–1860*. Urbana and Chicago: University of Illinois Press, 1979.
U.S. Fish and Wildlife Service. "Passengers of the *Steamboat Bertrand*: Fannie and Annie Campbell" (brochure). https://www.fws.gov.
———. "Passengers of the *Steamboat Bertrand*: The Atchison Family" (brochure). https://www.fws.gov.
Valvano, Christopher F. "Missouri Workhorse: The Boats, Business and Backs of St. Charles, Missouri." Master's thesis, East Carolina University, 2017.

Bibliography

Van Cleve, Paul., "Longest Steamboat Race." *Billings (MT) Gazette*, March 27, 1966.

Vicksburg American. July 1, 1909.

Vogel, Kristen Marie. "'It Wasn't the Money Boat': The Myth and Reality of Treasure Hunting in Western River Steamboats in the United States." PhD dissertation, Texas A&M University, 2017.

The War of the Rebellion: A Compilation of the Official Records of the Union and Confederate Armies (128 vols.). Washington, D.C.: United States Government Printing Office, 1880–1901.

Washington (DC) Sentinel. "Affray on Western Steamboat Suicide by Drowning." October 25, 1853.

Washington (KS) Register. January 26, 1884.

Washington (MO) Citizen. "Big Dredge Boat '*Kappa*' Is Sunk." March 21, 1930.

———. "Snagboat Burns Near Gasconade." August 3, 1928.

———. "St. Louis Man Furnishes More Information on Old Ferry Boat." September 13, 1964.

———. "3,000 Steamers Once Operated on Old Muddy." November 15, 1964.

Washington (MO) Missourian. "Confederate Raiders Attack South Point and Washington." October 15, 1964.

———. "Part of Washington's Early History." September 22, 1960.

Waterways Journal. August 22, 1953.

Way, Frederick Way, Jr. *Way's Packet Directory, 1848–1994.* Revised paperback edition. Athens: Ohio University Press, 1994.

Western Watchman (St. Louis MO). "The Steamboat Disaster." June 6, 1850.

Wheeling Daily Intelligencer. November 24, 1864.

INDEX

A

Arabia 9, 11, 135, 137, 138, 139, 140, 141, 142, 143, 146

B

Ballard, Henry 55, 57, 58
Barrows, Willard 129, 131, 132, 147
Belt, Francis 53, 54, 55, 56, 57
Bennett, Bill 133
Benton (No. 2) 94, 95, 104, 105
Bertrand 11, 26, 28, 120, 127, 128, 129, 130, 131, 132, 133, 134, 139
Big Hatchie 50, 101
Bixby, Horace 128, 129, 130
Blackburn, Jonathan 54, 56
Boland, James 104, 105
Boreas 64, 126
Bright Star 86, 87
Brockman, Ferdinand 54, 56, 57

C

Cataract 52, 53
Chittenden, Hiram Martin 37, 115, 118, 122, 123
Clancy, Josiah 54, 56, 57
Clark, John 87, 88
Conrad, Peter 53, 54, 58
Cora Island 68, 120
Cora (No. 1) 120, 132
Cora (No. 2) 66, 120
Corbino, Sam 133, 134, 139

D

Dacotah 99, 104
Dickens, Charles 23, 28, 145
Dodd, Henry 112, 113, 114
Dunbar, William 56, 57, 58

E

Edna 49

Index

Edward Bates 63, 64
Effie Deans 117, 118
El Paso 101
Emilie 101, 116, 117
Emilie LaBarge 118
Expedition 20

F

Fannie Ogden 120
Far West 109, 110, 111, 114
Fitch, George 29, 33

G

Galvanized Yankees 89
General Meade 91, 113
Great St. Louis Fire 52, 63, 65, 116
Guerette, Louis 54, 57

H

Hawley, David 139, 140, 143
Hawley, Greg 139, 141, 142, 143
Heckman, William ("Steamboat Bill") 97, 122
Henry, William 78, 81, 83, 84, 85
Henson, Gale 138
Hermann 22, 46
Hunter, Louis 26, 33, 36, 38, 123

I

Independence 18, 19, 20

J

James Monroe 73
Jefferson 20

J.M. Clendenin 91, 92
Joe Kinney 120
John Golong 126, 143
Judith 93

K

Kappa 46, 48
Kate Kinney (No. 1) 120
Kate Kinney (No. 2) 120
Keith, George 98, 101, 102
Kinney, Cora 66
Kinney, Joseph 66, 118, 120, 121

L

LaBarge, Charles 54, 56, 114
LaBarge, Joseph 71, 72, 101, 113, 114, 115, 116, 117, 118, 122, 123
Lady Lee 93, 94
Lass, William E. 99, 123
Long, Major Stephen 19, 20
Luella 108, 109

M

Mars 89
Marsh, Grant 100, 107, 108, 109, 110, 111, 112, 114, 123
Massie, William Rodney 101, 102, 104, 109, 112, 122, 123, 144
Mattie Bell 94
McFadden, Alexander 59
McFadden, George C. 59
Missouri 46, 48, 114
Mollie Dozier 41, 42, 43, 44
Montana 99, 100, 101, 102, 104
Moselle 36

INDEX

N

New Lucy 44, 45, 46
New Sam Gaty 78, 79, 80, 81, 83, 84, 85, 132

P

Polar Star 45
Pontiac 126
Price, Sterling 86, 92, 117
Pursell, Jesse 133, 134, 139

Q

Quarantine Island 73, 74

R

Rivercene 121
River Salvage Inc. 135, 137, 140, 141, 142, 143, 144, 145
R.W. Dugan 120

S

Saluda 37, 53, 54, 55, 56, 57, 59, 61, 114
Sam Gaty 79, 85
Sargent, John 57, 58, 61
Schuttner, Eberhardt 78, 81, 83, 84, 85
Shrader, Dorothy Heckman 122
Sisk, Gary 139, 144, 145, 146
Smith, Gene 139, 145
Sortor, Norman 139, 140, 142
Spread Eagle 101, 102
St. Ange 72, 116
Steamboat Act of 1838 36, 50

Steamboat Act of 1852 36
St. Luke 97, 98, 99, 113, 120

T

T.F. Eckert 40, 102
Timour 52, 64
Tobener, Henry 137
Trail, E.B. 66, 114, 122
Treadway, Robert 137
Twain, Mark 27, 29, 108, 128
Twilight 144, 145, 146

W

Wabash Bridge (St. Charles, Missouri) 97, 98, 102, 113
Walsworth, F.D. 139
Western Engineer 19, 20, 25
West Wind 88, 89
Wheatley, William 127, 129, 130, 132
White Cloud 63, 64, 65
William H. Russell 118
Wiseman, Matilda 57, 58
Wm. J. Lewis 42, 43, 44

Y

Yellowstone 71, 115
Yore, James 128, 129, 130, 132, 134

ABOUT THE AUTHORS

Vicki Berger Erwin has written twenty-nine books in varied genres: picture books, middle-grade mysteries and novels, local histories and true crime. Her husband, James W. Erwin, has written only four previous books, three on the Civil War in Missouri and a history of St. Charles, Missouri. They owned a bookstore in St. Charles for eight years before they retired.

Vicki and Jim met in the Ellis Library at the University of Missouri–Columbia, they checked each other out and the rest is history. They live in Kirkwood, Missouri. This is their first book together.

Visit us at
www.historypress.com